Mountain Biking New Hampshire's

STATE PARKS AND FORESTS

Mountain Biking New Hampshire's
STATE PARKS AND FORESTS

LINDA CHESTNEY

NICOLIN FIELDS
PUBLISHING

27 Dearborn Ave., Hampton, NH 03842 (603) 926-4581

Library of Congress Cataloging-in-Publication Data

Chestney, Linda, 1952–
    Mountain biking New Hampshire's state parks and forests / Linda Chestney. -- 1st ed.
      p.   cm.
    ISBN 0-9637077-3-6 (pbk. : alk. paper)
    1. All terrain cycling--New Hampshire--Guidebooks. 2. New Hampshire--Guidebooks.   I. Title.
GV1045.5.N4C477 1996
796.6'4'09742--dc20

                                95-50711
                                CIP

Cover design by Bob Jolin, © 1996 Nicolin Fields Publishing
Maps by R.P. Hale, © 1996 Nicolin Fields Publishing
Photos by author, except when noted otherwise.

First Edition/First Printing

To the light of my life,
the wind at my back,
the pearl among the pebbles,
my husband,
Al Blake.

ACKNOWLEDGMENTS

An incredible amount of effort, time and energy goes into the creation of a book. And even though it's an individual project as a whole, the reality is that many people are a part of making it happen. Without them, the quality, detail and expertise of the final product would suffer. So with my ever-indebted gratitude, I thank the following people for their integral part in making this book a reality.

Many thanks to my patron, Brad Hill, owner of Goodale's Bike and Ski, Inc. in Nashua, New Hampshire, for his enthusiastic support and unflagging effort to secure Giant mountain bikes, equipment and clothing for this book project. Thanks to Goodale's staff. A class-act bunch. Thanks also to Giant for its generosity and support of this book, and indirectly, mountain biking in New Hampshire.

Thanks to Granite State Wheelman, New Hampshire's premier bicycling organization. Thanks also to GSW's founder, faithful leader and worker, Dave Topham, whose dedication to bicycling has made a profound difference.

This book owes its existence to all of the people who helped "behind the scenery" researching trails and selflessly giving their time and expertise. Many ride researchers know the areas they explored far better than most—because the areas they researched are, figuratively speaking, in their back yard. Thanks, guys!

Roger Turner	Mike Micucci
Fred McLaughlin	Ellen Chandler
Cheryl Phillips	Liz Sterns
James McDonough	Sue Drew
Stuart McDonough	Steve Langella
Bob MacGregor	Mike Stewart
David Robichaud	Kathy Downes
Scott Curtis	Dick Hodgkinson
Steve McGrath	Louise McCleery

Also I'm beyond-words grateful to the super people from the New Hampshire Department of Resources and Economic Development. This includes the Division of Forests and Lands, and the Division of Parks and Recreation.

Specifically, I'd like to say thank you to Program Specialist for the Parks Trails Bureau, Bob Spoerl, who tirelessly, graciously answered my zillion questions, scouted down maps and generously shared his wealth of knowledge, and provided me with boxes of research information. Thanks, too, to Jane Mammone and Sarah Durgin, who picked up the slack for Bob when he was "in the field." Thanks to Alan Smith for his expertise and input. My gratitude to Allison McLean for her eye for detail.

My thanks especially to the forestry guys. Thanks to Jim Carter, Land Management Administrator. And to the foresters who knew the forest trails like the backs of their hands—Dan DeHart, J.B. Cullen, Howard Lewis, Tom Miner, Ray Boivin, Bob MacGregor, Mike Stewart and Doug Miner.

But my favorite foresters were the ones who spent time with me "in the field" to facilitate this project and make it the best possible. My heartfelt thanks to Shaun Bresnahan, Bob Hardy and Rick Spafford. Exploring the rocky trails, investigating tombstones dating back to the 1700s, having lunch by a bog where a Great Blue Heron fished nearby and digging a pick-up truck out of the mud—all will be memories I'll take with me from this summer. Thanks, guys. You're a special breed.

Thanks, too, to my family who supported me through this project. The frantic days of "Will I ever get this done on deadline?" Thanks Jason, Amy. Thanks, Al, my husband and "balancer." Thanks to my extended family in Iowa, South Dakota and throughout the upper Midwest. And thanks, too, to Al's wonderful family, and the NML family.

Thanks to God for being ever-present.

*Detailed maps of each state park
or forest are in individual chapters.*

Trail
Locations

Nash Stream
Forest
①

Success
Pond
②

Moose Brook
State Park ③
④ Lead Mine
State Forest

Franconia Notch
⑤ State Park

⑥ Black Mountain
State Forest

Hemenway
State Forest ⑦

Heath Pond Bog
Natural Area ⑩

Pine River ⑪
State Forest

Wade
State Forest
⑨

Gile
State Forest

Franklin Falls
Reservoir

⑧

Sugar River
Rail Trail

⑫

State Forest Nursery

Rollins & Winslow
State Parks

⑯

⑮ ⑭ ⑬

Blackwater Reservoir

Dodge Brook State Forest

Pillsbury
⑳ State Park

Mast Yards
State Forest

Northwood
Meadows
State Park

Honey Brook
State Forest ㉒ ㉓

⑰

㉑

Fox Forest ㉔ ⑲

㉕

㉗

Pawtuckaway
㉘ State Park

Totten Trails State Forest

⑱ ㉖

Bear
Brook S.P.

㉙

Odiorne
Point
State Park

Vincent State Forest

Hopkinton-
Everett
Reservoir

㉛ Rockingham
Recreation
Trail

Clough
State Park

Pisgah
State Park

㉜

Annett
State Forest

Litchfield
㉚ State Forest

Hale

㉝

㉞ Russell-Abbott
State Forest

N

TABLE OF CONTENTS

INTRODUCTION

Uniquely New Hampshire

What's your preference? Would you rather travel the intricate network of bike trails in Franconia Notch or the 10-mile Sugar River Trail where two of only five remaining historical covered railroad bridges in the U.S. reside? Or would you choose a pine needle-covered trail in one of the state forests where the sun throws a dappled pattern across your path and the smell of pitch is intoxicating? This book offers all of those choices and more. It's your decision. But rest assured, whatever your choice, it's a right one.

New Hampshire has nearly *too much* to offer—the forests, mountains, seashore. But the diversity within the state is one of its greatest assets. And all of these areas have something to offer the person interested in mountain biking. The trails in New Hampshire are endless. We're fortunate to have both a New Hampshire Division of Parks and Recreation, and a Division of Forests and Lands that are extremely supportive of this sport.

Based on the controversy over mountain biking in the West, specifically California, I expected some resistance or at the very least reluctance from the state parks and forestry people when I began this project. My anticipation was entirely off-base. I never encountered one person who was the least bit hesitant to offer assistance. On the contrary, I found immense support and encouragement. I heard frequently, especially about the forests, "New Hampshire has wonderful natural resources available for the public to enjoy. We just wish there was a way to get more people here to appreciate them."

Well, here's the way. But remember, along with the privilege of exploring mountain bike trails in New Hampshire's state forests and parklands, comes responsibility. Please respect the land. That means carry your trash out with you. Respect the wildlife—leave it alone. Don't encourage land erosion by skidding your bike and displacing the earth. Don't go on private property without permission. Be courteous to others you meet on the trails, and pedal softly.

If we treat the parklands and forests with respect, it will ensure that the privilege of using and enjoying these state public properties will remain for our children's children and generations to come. Consider volunteering—help maintain the trails you use. Give back a bit of what nature gives you.

So ride, enjoy and respect just what you expect from New Hampshire—beautiful wilderness and classic New England scenery.

Biking Tips

This book is for the leisure mountain bike rider—the family or weekend rider. The rides tend to be more the beginner and intermediate level than the expert rider, although numerous trails also qualify as expert. But for the most part you need not be concerned with the "carry-your-bike-up-the-ledge-and-bushwhack-for-the-next-half-mile" kind of trails. It's for the fun of riding and the appreciation of nature. That doesn't mean you can't get some long rides in—you definitely can. Read the ride descriptions for each park, forest or nature area and decide from there.

I can't promise there won't be changes from what has been recorded in the book. Nature changes constantly, and we must be willing to accommodate the change. A pine tree may fall across the path. A logging company may create a new spur road. A spring thaw may cause a stream across the path that wasn't there when the trails were mapped. Go with the flow and have flexible expectations.

Just Be Nice...

Here are some paraphrased suggestions concerning a code of behavior offered by NORBA, the National Off-Road Bicycle Association:

14

ଔ Yield the right-of-way to other non-motorized recreationists. People will judge all cyclists by your behavior.

ଔ Slow down when approaching other cyclists, walkers or equestrians. Let them know *in advance* that you're approaching—call out, "Hello there."

ଔ Ride under control. Be cautious going around bends—someone may be there.

ଔ Stay on designated trails to avoid trampling vegetation and to minimize trail erosion—stay off them during the spring mud season. The reason for avoiding trails when they are wet, is that tires leave ruts which then causes runoff erosion. Save it for a sunny day.

ଔ Don't disturb wildlife or livestock.

ଔ Don't litter. What you carry in, carry out. Be a good do-bee—pick up other people's trash.

ଔ Respect public *and* private property. Obey trail signs and "No Trespassing" signs.

ଔ Wear a helmet when you ride. Use your head—it could save your life.

Equipment

What do you need to go mountain biking for the day? The following items are highly recommended. Don't ignore this list, feeling you're invincible. Pay attention—your life could depend on it.

ଔ **Bike.** Obviously this is a basic. Get advice from a reputable bike shop on what's best for your riding needs. And make sure you get a comfortable seat. Mount a pump on your bike in case you have a flat tire.

ଔ **Bike Bag.** To carry various equipment—a spare tube, tire levers, grease rags, first-aid kit, spoke wrench, compass, allen wrenches, lunch. This could be a handle bar-mounted bag with a clear-plastic map pouch on top.

ᐅ **Water.** Bring along a minimum of two large bottles. Plan for more than you'll think you'll need. Sip water often. Even when you're not thirsty.

ᐅ **Odometer (computer).** These handy gadgets help you know how far you've gone. It parallels the map's mileage, also helps you stay oriented in the wilderness.

ᐅ **Clothing.** Dress comfortably. Avoid blue jeans. Try Lycra riding shorts or something that is comfortable. You can buy shorts with chamois or gel seats. It could make a difference between a super ride or one where you suffer saddle sores. Buy bike shoes for support and comfort. A rain poncho is a good idea in case you get caught in the rain.

ᐅ **Bug spray.** Early in the spring you may need this. Although if you don't stop a lot, the bugs should leave you alone. You're going faster than they are.

ᐅ **Maps.** The more maps you have of an area, the better. Local gazetteers and atlases are good resources. But probably topping the heap are the USGS maps (United States Geological Survey). These "topo" (topographical) maps show contours/elevations of land. It's handy to understand how much you'll be climbing. Many bike shops now carry topo maps of their area. A large town library or a university library would probably carry them also. Photocopy what you need and bring it on the ride.

Mountain Biking in New Hampshire's Parklands

The state of New Hampshire welcomes mountain bikers to its parklands and trails. Most of the state parks, trails, forests, rails-to-trails routes, and natural areas are open to mountain bike use. Some trails are closed, however, for safety or environmental reasons. Trails closed to mountain biking have signs posted with the diagonal slash through a bike indicating "No Bikes." Most of the state park trails are closed during the spring mud season.

Many of the state parks charge admission during the main season, which runs from Memorial Day weekend through mid-June on weekends only; from then until Labor Day, parks are open on a daily basis. The per-person rate is $2.50. Children under 12 with their family are admitted free. Frequent park users may purchase discount coupon books or summer season passes.

Camping and open fires are not allowed in state parks except in designated areas. A carry-in, carry-out policy is in effect at all state parks and forests. The trash barrels have been removed from these parks. So please, carry out whatever you've carried in. This program also encourages area wildlife to remain wild by eliminating the availability of food scraps. Additionally, the wildlife are protected from the hidden dangers typically found in our trash. For instance, plastic six-pack holders and fishing line.

Friends of the Parks

Friends of the Parks are numerous nonprofit groups that raise money, build trails, prepare exhibits, conduct special programs or provide similar services for New Hampshire state parks. Their efforts enrich and enhance visitors' experiences. If you would like to join or form a "Friends of the Parks" group or just want additional information, contact the New Hampshire Division of Parks and Recreation at (603) 271-3254.

Individuals can also make a meaningful contribution as a state park volunteer. Volunteers perform a variety of tasks, from maintaining facilities to restoring historic artifacts. Most donate an occasional Saturday or weekend. Those with special skills may give talks or conduct tours in their areas of expertise. If you are interested in becoming a state park volunteer, contact the Division of Parks and Recreation at (603) 271-3254 or talk with a local state park manager.

New Hampshire State Forests

New Hampshire is one of the most densely forested states in the U.S. Forest covers 87 percent of the state—just as it did three centuries ago. As a renewable resource, forests are critical to the economy of the state.

The forest industry is the oldest land-based industry in New Hampshire—and no other industry better exemplifies the independent Yankee spirit. It began in 1634 when the first virgin pines were sent to England as masts for the Royal Navy. Two decades later, the king decreed all trees over 24 inches in diameter were the property of England. It is said that New Hampshire patriots joined the Revolution not over tea and taxes, but to protect their timber supply.

17

Today the forest industry is New Hampshire's third largest manufacturing industry, and the foundation of this state's rural economy. The forest provides a wide variety of goods and is a source of aesthetic and recreational enjoyment, habitat for wildlife, and is a natural filter assuring water quality.

A large portion of our forests (84 percent) are owned by private citizens and the forest industry. Forestry provides income to private landowners so that they can continue to own their land, keep it green and scenic, and open for responsible public use.

Although New Hampshire has hundreds of thousands of acres in its 112 state forests, not all of them are appropriate for mountain biking. Some forests, such as Low State Forest in Bradford, are not appropriate for mountain biking because the trails are too rocky or steep. We'll save those areas for hiking. But we've uncovered so many wonderful forest trails that were unmapped before now, that it'll take awhile for you to cover them all, if that's your goal.

Forests are unlike most state parks, however, in that they may not be readily identified with a sign announcing the forest. There may not be a picnic area or a ranger station. It may simply be trees. So pay attention to the route notes in the chapters ahead to help you identify where you need to go to find the forests.

One clue that you're on forest property is that the boundaries are marked with blue paint on trees along the way. Many of the trails in this book will take you off the forest property, but still keep you on public land—gravel town roads, for example. They may have occasional vehicle traffic or none, but they are available for mountain bike use.

Camping and campfires should be by permission of the park or foresters only, and then only in designated safe areas. Remember that logging trucks always have the right of way. (Who'd want to take one on anyway?) If you've secured permission to ride on private property, use your manners and thank the landowner. This small gesture will do much to ensure that the privilege is there next year.

Before You Hit the Trail

So that you better understand how this book can best help you, please read the next section before you go cruising on your bike for the day. *Mountain Biking New Hampshire's State Parks and Forests* groups rides in three categories based on difficulty. Beginner, intermediate and advanced.

Beginner (novice) rides are the least difficult. Very appropriate for a family outing. Often these rides also have picnic areas, swimming holes and other recreational activities nearby. The riding tends to be on basically flat roads with few obstructions.

Intermediate rides offer more challenge. Perhaps rockier terrain, maybe some water bars to cross over, a stream to ford or some pushing your bike uphill. Not necessarily to be avoided. If it's too hard to ride, get off and walk. Sometimes you appreciate nature better if you're passing at a slower pace.

Advanced rides require more skill, a stronger, more experienced rider. Better balance and stamina. The ability to navigate steeper hills or climb upward for a sustained time. Or to carry a bike over a rocky area or splash through a water bar.

Don't discount a ride because it's advanced. The panoramic view might be worth the work. Also, there's no shame in walking or pushing your bike for a ways. You're out there getting exercise. That counts for something! Also, bear in mind that the ride levels defined here are guidelines. The ride that's fun and moderately challenging to one person may be very difficult for another—or possibly no challenge at all to the next. Carefully assess your skill level and don't take on more than you can comfortably handle. Ride smart.

Posted Signs

You will see a number of different signs throughout the park system. Many designate appropriate trails for biking, hiking, snowmobiling, etc. Some signs restrict biking. Obey them or deal with the consequences. Signs banning motorized dirt bikes and all-terrain vehicles (ATVs), however, do not apply to mountain bikes.

Local Attractions

To further enhance your biking experience, this book also includes scenic and historic attractions in the area you're riding. Some areas obviously have more to offer than others. Enjoy your adventures.

Terminology

It will behoove you to understand a few words that are used to describe trails.

ATVs: All-terrain vehicles. In multi-purpose areas, you may be sharing the trails with ATVs.

Double-Track Road: Roads that are often frequented by four-wheel-drive, heavy-duty vehicles like Jeeps, Blazers, etc. You are apt to find rocks, tree roots, earth erosion here.

Hard Packed: Road or trail where dirt is packed hard. Super for moving along at a good pace. And if you wipe out, less painful than rocks.

Single-Track Road: Ummm. Much like double-track, but only one track. Often created by game animals (deer, moose) or from other bikers over the years. Weeds, rocks and roots may impede your progress.

Spur Road: These are side roads that have often been created by logging companies who have logged a region. The spur roads are often worth your while just because they're there.

Water Bar: A structure of earth (or other material such as wood or rock formations) which channel water off a trail.

Map Key:
Numbered Roads/paved

127

Gravel Roads
Stirrup Iron
Road

Trails
Clement Hill
Rd.

Northern Region

CHAPTER 1

NASH STREAM FOREST

Nash Stream Forest is in the hinterlands of New Hampshire. The North Country. But it may well be worth the drive. These trails are, for the most part, for the advanced rider. But a trail or two is appropriate for a beginner or intermediate rider who may not mind walking a bit. Exceptional scenic mountain views of Percy Peaks and Sugarloaf Mountain abound. You'll meet very few other bikers or vehicle traffic. An abundance of wildlife keeps you in awe. And the fresh air is invigorating. Sounds like a good bet.

Nash Stream Forest is a 39,601-acre tract of land owned by the state of New Hampshire and managed by the Department of Resources and Economic Development. It lies within a four-state region known as the Northern Forest that stretches from the coast of Maine, across northern New Hampshire and Vermont into New York, totaling 26 million acres. Its acquisition in 1988 was a collaborative effort by the state of New Hampshire, the U.S. Forest Service, The Nature Conservancy, the Trust for New Hampshire Lands, and the Society for the Protection of New Hampshire Forests. The Northern Forest is one of the largest expanses of continuously forested land in the nation with about 85 percent in private ownership. Forest-based economies, recreation and environmental diversity are traditional to the areas as are clean air and water.

Nash Stream Forest has no visitors' center or gate keeper. But the property is open for public use. All-terrain vehicles (ATVs) and trail bikes are not permitted, but mountain biking is allowed on established roads and trails unless posted otherwise. There is no entry fee.

Plants and Wildlife

Nash Stream Forest is home to five rare plant species: black crowberry, marsh horsetail, three-forked rush, broad-lipped twayblade and millet grass. Four of the five are listed as threatened by the New Hampshire Native Plant Protection Act. The other, three-forked rush, is relatively rare, but not state-listed.

No federally listed animal species are known to breed on the property. Peregrine falcons and bald eagles nest within 20 miles of the property and are frequently seen in the forest. Common loons and northern harriers have nested in the area for several years. Lynx and marten wander through but are not residents of the forest. You're apt to see moose early in the morning. Pileated woodpeckers and song birds dart about. If your timing is right, you could be escorted throughout your ride by thousands of black and yellow tiger swallowtail butterflies. They emerge late spring, early summer.

Ride Information

Ride Level:	Some beginner trails. Mostly very advanced.
Trail Distances:	Vary. Can do a short run or as long as 22 miles round trip out Nash Stream Road to 19½ Road and back to parking area.
Trail Descriptions:	Gravel roads, some double- and some single-track trails. Muddy in the spring.
Highlights:	Not much up here for tourist-type attractions, but the vistas of natural beauty you'll encounter far transcend any human-created entertainment. Picnic spot at Pond Brook Falls, swimming holes.
Start:	From Route 3 in Groveton, take Route 110 east for 2 miles, turn left on Emerson Road. Drive 2.1 miles to Nash Stream Road. Turn left on this gravel road for half a mile to the forest property. Park at the main gate. A large map is posted here.
Note:	This area has a short riding season because it's very muddy and wet in the spring. Late fall is deer hunting season.

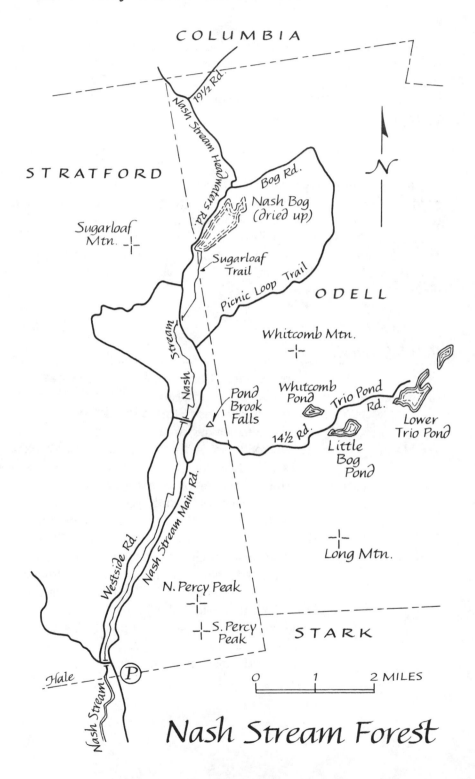

COLUMBIA

STRATFORD

19½ Rd.

Nash Stream Headwaters Rd.

Bog Rd.

Nash Bog
(dried up)

Sugarloaf
Mtn.

Sugarloaf
Trail

Picnic Loop Trail

ODELL

N

Whitcomb Mtn.

Nash Stream

Pond
Brook
Falls

Whitcomb
Pond

Trio Pond Rd.

Lower
Trio Pond

14½ Rd.

Little
Bog
Pond

Long Mtn.

Westside Rd.

Nash Stream Main Rd.

N. Percy Peak

S. Percy
Peak

STARK

Hale

P

0   1   2 MILES

Nash Stream

Nash Stream Forest

Ride Options

1. West Side Road. An exceptionally scenic, easy ride. The rolling gravel road offers great views downstream toward Percy Peaks. It can be done as a loop, but you would need to wade a stream. To do a loop: 5 miles in on West Side Road an old log-landing exists. Take the right road. It plunges steeply down to the river. Cross to the camp and out the driveway, you'll come out just past Pond Brook Falls. Then it's a quick cruise to the gate. Do this loop counter clockwise, if you'd like to see breathtaking views ahead of you. If you go counter clockwise, you will need to carry your bike from Nash Stream to West Side Road.

2. The Trio Ponds. Fun route if you like a more "technical" ride. (For you rookies, that means, "Don't try it!") This area is a favorite for the advanced rider. $14\frac{1}{2}$ Road is a very tough climb and a "high-speed screamer" coming out. Watch for uphill traffic.

3. Nash Bog loop. A clockwise loop of Nash Bog—following Picnic Loop Trail is challenging. Nash Bog has been bone dry the last couple of summers, so you may only see crackled mud where the bog used to be. You climb from Bog Road to East Branch Road and you'll carry your bike at times. A great ride for the prepared, gritty mountain biker.

4. Nash Stream Road. Meanders along Nash Stream. It is a gravel road that has occasional road traffic. The road is super for mountain biking. Swimming holes are to your left as you travel beside the stream. Dramatic cliffs form a backdrop. You'll have a moderate climb at the beginning of the road, but hills are few and views frequent.

5. Pond Brook Falls. The perfect picnic spot. Continue up Nash Stream Road from the $14\frac{1}{2}$ Road, through a gate. Follow Pond Brook to the waterfalls. Great for swimming, too. Just be careful of the water current.

6. $19\frac{1}{2}$ Road. At the far end (north) of Nash Stream Road. It splits to the right before the gate. It is said that $19\frac{1}{2}$ Road hooks up with Phillips Pond, which in turn connects east to the Androscoggin River and hundreds of square miles of pristine, remote wilderness.

7. Other Rides. If you are a rugged individualist in super physical shape, have great stamina and want a challenge, pick up Steve Langella's book, *Mountain Bike Steve's Wilderness Treks* (or send for it—see address at the end of Chapter 3). Steve outlines 19 trail rides in the Nash Stream area.

CHAPTER 2

SUCCESS POND

T he North Country. That's what this remote area of New Hampshire is called. It's an unspoiled part of our state that has every intention of remaining that way. The Success Pond rides begin near the Androscoggin River, where once mammoth log drives headed for Berlin and Gorham jammed its waters. This river is now protected by a conservation easement. Along Route 16 that parallels the Androscoggin, are some of the most scenic drives in the state.

It's a nature lover's paradise. Birding is spectacular up here. Fishermen sing its praises (while trying to keep their lucky spot a secret), hikers head for Mount Success for a fabulous view, particularly from The Outlook. It's about halfway up the mountain and is a hanging ledge that offers a wide, panoramic view of the area. And then there are moose. Everywhere. Especially in the morning. Locals see them as commonly as the southern tier sees chipmunks.

Ride Information

Ride Level:	Intermediate and advanced.
Trail Distances:	28, 44 or 32 miles.
Trail Descriptions:	Firm gravel base. No washed out areas or obstacles to overcome. A few moguls on the road. Success Pond is an active logging road. Flat roads.

Highlights: Very isolated area. If you're into hiking, Mount Success offers a comprehensive view of the North Country from The Outlook. (Check an AMC Guide.) Numerous AMC trails are off Success Pond Road, should you want to combine your ride with a hike or two.

Start: From Hutchins Street in downtown Berlin, travel .7 mile to the OHRV area sign. Follow the signs a quarter of a mile to the parking area.

Note: This is a multi-purpose trail area. You may encounter ATVs here. Be careful.

Ride Options

1. Success Pond Road. This 28 mile out-and-back trip offers a firm gravel base and a flat road. Overhead 3,600-foot mountains loom. At the end of this 14-mile run is Success Pond. Mature bald eagles have been spotted here in the fall. They actually nest 15 miles north on Lake Umbagog. Also keep an eye out for pileated woodpeckers, flickers, moose, bobcat, bear and coyote.

If you have the energy on your return trip, you may want to investigate some of the many spur roads. Mark every intersection so you don't get lost. Also, it's a good opportunity to check out some of the AMC trailheads—maybe take a little hike.

2. OHRV Trail to Success Pond. This 44-mile out-and-back trail begins across from the OHRV parking area. Before you take off, take some time to familiarize yourself with the signage. The route is marked, but you'll need to pay attention to stay on the correct trail. This trail is shared with ATVs. Some dangerous stretches will be encountered on this trail. The single track becomes steep quickly and features loose rocks and lots of mud. After a mile or so you come across power lines. You'll cross a wood bridge and enter rolling, sandy terrain. Follow the OHRV signs and you'll intersect with Success Pond Road.

The trail continues, alternating between single track and logging roads until it breaks out of the forest 18 miles from the start. Continue on the marked OHRV trails and you'll arrive at Success Pond.

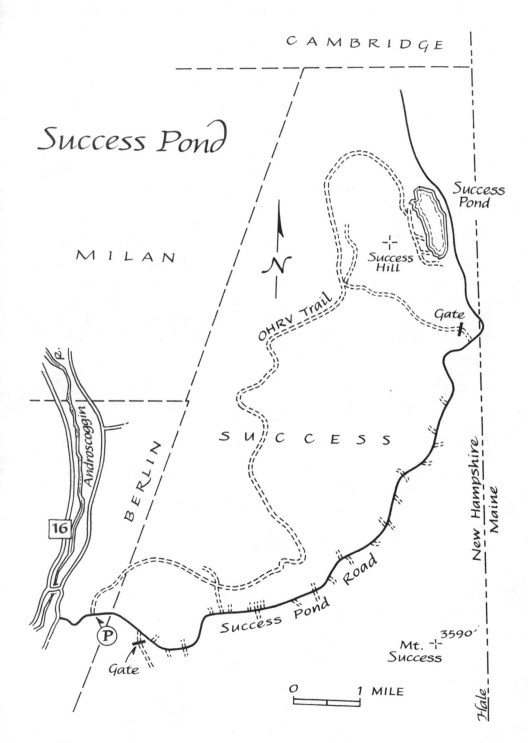

Success Pond

CAMBRIDGE

MILAN

Success Pond

Success Hill

OHRV Trail

N

SUCCESS

Gate

BERLIN

Androscoggin R.

16

New Hampshire
Maine

Success Pond Road

P

Gate

Mt. Success 3590'

Hale

0   1 MILE

3. Berlin to Success Pond Loop. Take either Success Pond Road or the OHRV trail and cross over to the other at Success Pond.

4. Success and beyond. If you're an expert rider and an adventurous type, you may want to explore the northern reaches of Cambridge, NH. If you travel far enough, you'll find that remote logging roads will crisscross their way from Success Pond to the Androscoggin River in Errol or to Lake Umbagog on the Maine border. But remember, according to one highly seasoned expert mountain biker who travels this area a lot, this is "die if you can't make it" territory.

5. Other rides. If you love this trail area, are in super physical shape, have great stamina and want a challenge, you might want to pick up Steve Langella's book, *Mountain Bike Steve's Wilderness Treks.* (Or order it by mail—the address is at the end of Chapter 3.) Steve outlines 19 trail rides in the Nash Stream area outside of Pittsburg, NH. Not for the faint of heart, but rather the rugged, more advanced biker.

MOOSE BROOK STATE PARK

L isten to the quiet. That's a lot of what you'll hear up north in Gorham, NH. Surrounded by the White Mountains, Moose Brook State Park near Berlin has terrific views south to the Presidential Range, highest mountains in the northeast. If mountain biking hasn't worn you out, hiking trails to the west and north offer the determined athlete a chance to conquer the less rugged Crescent or Randolph Ranges of the northern White Mountains.

The 755-acre park has a large natural outdoor pool (famous for its cold water), a small beach, bathhouse, picnic area and camping facilities. Trout fishing is superb here in Moose Brook, Perkins Brook or other nearby streams. Miles of mountain bike trails offer a fun day in the wilderness.

The trail system, originally established by the Civilian Conservation Corps, had grown in. But with the help of volunteers, including 158 students and 20 adults from the Gorham Middle School, the maze of trails available offers more fun than even Pavlov's rats could imagine. Some trails are still undergoing clearing, but most are open and passable. Park Manager Mike Stewart says, "Mountain biking in and around Moose Brook State Park is unlimited. It will soon become the mountain bike hot spot for seasoned mountain bikers."

You'll want to be a strong intermediate to expert rider to take on Moose Brook, however. Some uphill climbing, some rocks to navigate around and some streams to ford present more challenge than your quiet pine-needle-covered forest paths. Many trails are snowmobile

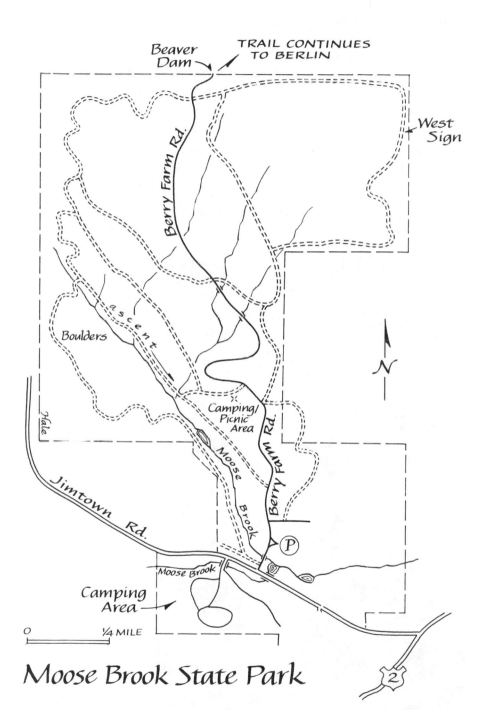

Beaver Dam

TRAIL CONTINUES TO BERLIN

West Sign

Berry Farm Rd.

ascent

Boulders

Hale

N

Camping/ Picnic Area

Moose Brook

Berry Farm Rd.

Jimtown Rd.

P

Moose Brook

Camping Area

0   ¼ MILE

Moose Brook State Park

2

trails and are not for the beginner rider. Trails on the right side of the map (east) are easier to handle than those on the left side (west). The trails on the west side of the park are more difficult snowmobile paths. Don't miss the beaver dam at the far end of Berry Farm Road.

Ride Information

Ride Level: Intermediate to expert.
Trail Distances: Varies. Can do a short 4-mile loop or as long as 20+ miles if you scout out all trails or extend your ride beyond the park to Berlin.

Keeping a map handy and checking it periodically helps assure that you won't get lost.

Al Blake

Trail Descriptions: Gravel road, some double- and single-track trails. Rugged at times. Steady uphills in some areas.

Highlights: Not much up here for tourist-type attractions, but nature has an advantage over contrived activities anyway. Picnic spot, swimming area, camping, beaver dam.

Start: Off U.S. Route 2, 2 miles west of Gorham. A sign announces the park entrance. Park in parking area.

Note: The main season runs from mid-May to mid-October. Fees for day use and camping. Moose Brook also offers an extended camping season through the self-service pay station. James River owns private logging property in this area. It's private land, so please stay off it.

Ride Options

1. East Loop. About 4 miles. Begin on Berry Farm Road, a maintained gravel road. Take the trail that goes to the right and circle back counter clockwise, hooking up with Berry Farm Road again, and eventually back to the parking area.

You'll face a moderate, but steady uphill climb for the first 2 miles until you see the trail sign that says "West." Soon you'll blend to the left where there are some stretches of grass and gravel on a double-track path. It's flat for awhile near the beaver dam. This side of the map (right side) has easier trails than the left.

2. West Loop. About 4.5 miles. This trail begins on Berry Farm Road. Take this gravel road to just before the beaver dam and take a left. You'll begin a descent, but for every down there's an up, and this one comes as you begin to parallel Moose Brook. Soon you'll intersect with Berry Farm Road again and back to the parking lot.

3. Far West Trails. The trails on the far side of this map (left side) are the snowmobile paths. Far more technical and no fun if you're out for a Sunday afternoon leisure ride. Unless you're an advanced rider or enjoy navigating around boulders, save them for another time.

4. Berry Farm Road to Berlin. If you're driven or have lots of time on your hands, you might want to follow Berry Farm Road out beyond where we've mapped. It will eventually bring you into Berlin.

5. Other rides. If you love these trails, and are in super physical shape, and want more terrain like this, pick up Steve Langella's book, *Mountain Bike Steve's Wilderness Treks* (or order by mail from Nicolin Fields Publishing, 27 Dearborn Ave., Hampton, NH 03842. The book is $17.95 ppd.). Steve outlines 19 trail rides a bit farther north in the Nash Stream area outside of Pittsburg, NH, that will challenge you. Highly skilled riders only.

CHAPTER 4

LEAD MINE STATE FOREST

Lead Mine State Forest is a short ride from Mascot Mine Natural Area. And that's where we're headed. This former lead and silver mine employed 60 workers in its heyday. Its dark shafts that reached down to the river now house five species of bats who have laid claim to the abandoned mines for their winter home.

This out-and-back 8.4-mile ride, which begins in Gorham and crosses into Shelburne, follows the hard-working Androscoggin River, a river which powers large paper mills in Berlin, NH and Gorham, ME. Along this stretch of the river, however, it's peaceful and beautiful.

This trip combines evidence of both human history and natural beauty. Lead Mine State Forest is on land formerly belonging to Anne Whitney, a noted Boston sculptress and abolitionist. The ride travels through large hemlock and oak stands, both rare in Coos County, and parallels the Androscoggin. Some paper birches, notable for their dazzling white bark, appear near the mine site. Many spectacular vistas of the Presidential Range grace this route. If you hike up to the mine entrance, you'll be rewarded with tremendous views of Mount Madison, Mount Washington, Pinkham Notch and the Carter Range.

This ride is near Nash Stream, Success Pond and Moose Brook State Park, previously mentioned in this book. You may want to combine several rides in New Hampshire's North Country since you're in the area already.

Ride Information

Ride Level:	Intermediate to expert.
Trail Distances:	8.4 miles out and back.
Trail Descriptions:	Town-maintained gravel road generally flat. Last .7 of a mile before the mine is steep uphill with loose rocks.
Highlights:	Superb views of the Presidential Range, mine area, river for swimming.
Start:	In Gorham, from intersection of Route 2 and 16 (south), take Route 2 east for 3.5 miles, just after stone buildings on left, take a left on North Road. Take North Road across bridge. First left after bridge is Hogan Road. Park at intersection of Hogan and North Road or at Appalachian trailhead .3 miles down Hogan Road.
Note:	The mine site is a valuable nesting area for the five bat species who inhabit it. Please respect the gates on the mine and do not attempt to enter. If you're here during the hunting season, wear hunter orange. There is no charge to enter Lead Mine State Forest or Mascot Mine Natural Area. Please stay on the designated trail as much of this ride is on private land.

Ride Options

1. Lead Mine State Forest to Mascot Mine Natural Area. This is an out-and-back 8.4-mile ride. From the parking area follow Hogan Road. At .3 of a mile the Appalachian Trail leads to the right, stay left. At .9 miles there is a road to the right, stay left. At 1.2 miles another road goes to the right, stay left. At 1.3 miles you cross a wooden bridge.

At 1.4 miles, overlooking a gravel pit, is a great view of Mount Madison. At the Y at 2.5 miles, stay left. If you hit the right season, a blackberry patch on the left here offers succulent treats. At 2.9 miles is a left turn that goes to a power dam, stay right. At 3.5 miles you cross under a power line. Just past the power line take a right turn onto a gravel road. The gravel road ascends steeply and at 3.6 miles crosses back

Lead Mine State Forest

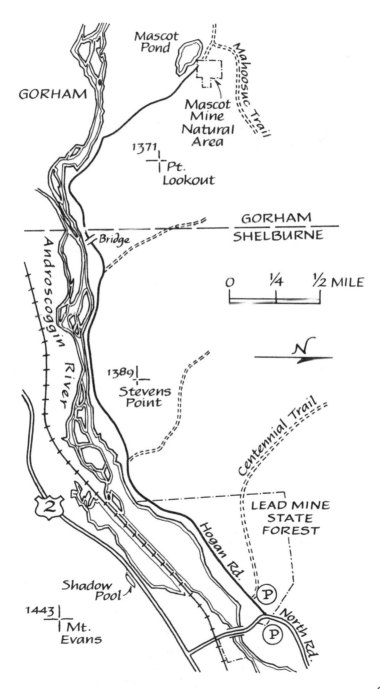

Mascot Pond

GORHAM

Mascot Mine Natural Area

Mahoosuc Trail

1371 Pt. Lookout

Bridge

GORHAM
SHELBURNE

0   ¼   ½ MILE

N

Androscoggin River

1389 Stevens Point

Centennial Trail

LEAD MINE STATE FOREST

2

Hogan Rd.

Shadow Pool

1443 Mt. Evans

P

P

North Rd.

under the power lines. Soon you'll reach a steep, rocky section sure to test your ability. Don't hesitate to walk.

At 4.2 miles you cross a red property line onto Mascot Mine Natural Area. Shortly you'll see Mascot Pond. The mine is on the ledge to the right. It is a steep hike up to the mine entrance, but is worth the hike as it provides tremendous views of the town of Gorham, Mount Madison and Washington, Pinkham Notch and the Carter range. Return the way you came.

2. Nearby. If you want to do more exploring, check out the three previous rides in the book—Nash Stream, Success Pond and Moose Brook State Park. They're all nearby.

CHAPTER 5

FRANCONIA NOTCH
STATE PARK

Touted as one of the 12 best state parks in the entire country by *Money Magazine*, Franconia Notch State Park is a spectacular mountain pass that extends from the Flume at the south end to Echo Lake at the north end. Sandwiched between the Franconia and Kinsman mountain ranges, Franconia Notch is truly one of America's outstanding parkways. The home of the famous Old Man of the Mountain, the same Great Stone Face immortalized by Nathaniel Hawthorne and Daniel Webster, the area offers various activities—hiking, biking, sight-seeing, camping, a ski museum, fly fishing, rock climbing, tramway rides and bird watching to name several. Other sights are mentioned below.

The bike ride is a gradual accent/descent of 21.2 miles over a paved trail if you go from one end to the other and back. (You can choose to go fewer miles and turn around whenever.) Views are perhaps the best in the state, including the Old Man of the Mountain and Profile Lake. You may want to take an hour tour of the Flume Gorge to see the river's 70-foot deep rock walls and waterfalls. There is a $6. fee to tour the Flume Gorge.

The bike trail, referred to in the park materials as the Franconia Notch Recreation Path, travels the entire length of Franconia Notch. You can park at various parking areas along Franconia Notch Parkway (I-93). Ride instructions begin at the southern trailhead at the Flume parking lot.

Flume Gorge

Discovered in 1808, the Flume Gorge is a natural gorge extending 800 feet at the base of Mount Liberty. The walls of Conway granite rise perpendicularly to a height of 70 to 90 feet and are from 12 to 20 feet apart. Bus service is available to transport visitors (or you can walk the trail) to the gorge entrance. Walking-trail signs explaining natural features lead to other points of interest, including the Pool and Sentinel Pine Bridge.

The newly constructed contemporary-style visitor center frames a spectacular vista of Mountain Liberty and the Flume. The structure also houses a cafeteria, gift shop and an auditorium where a video about the Notch is presented. Phone 603 745-8391.

The Basin

The beautiful waterfall at this site has a granite pothole at its base that is 20 feet in diameter. It is believed to have been eroded 15,000 years ago while the North American ice sheet was melting and has been smoothed by small stones and sand whirled around by the Pemigewasset River. Below the Basin is a water-eroded rock formation called the Old Man's Foot.

Boise Rock

In the early 1800s, Thomas Boise sought shelter under this large boulder when a blizzard blocked passage for him and his horse on the notch road. Near the boulder you can find a cool spring, picnic tables and an exceptional view of Cannon Cliffs.

Lafayette Place

The camping and hiking hub of the notch is centrally located in the park at Lafayette Place. Lafayette Campground provides 97 wooded tent sites, and regularly scheduled interpretive programs. To reserve camping space, call 603 271-3627. A lodge houses a registration desk and showers. Information about hiking trails, safety, and the natural and cultural history of the park is available in the visitor center cabin near the campground entrance. Phone 603 823-9513.

Profile Lake

This small, clear body of water is the headwaters of the Pemigewasset River. Directly below the Old Man of the Mountain, it is often called the

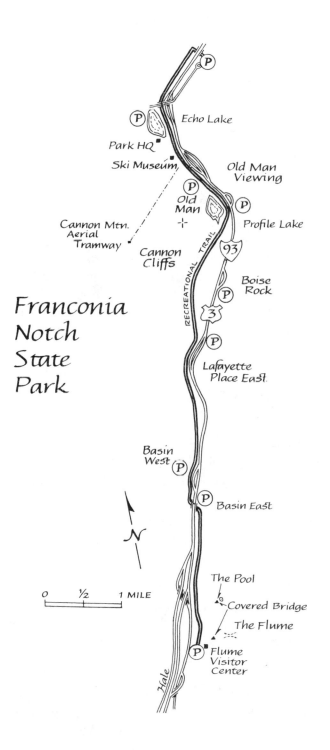

P

P Echo Lake

Park HQ

Ski Museum

Old Man
Viewing

P

Old Man

P

Profile Lake

Cannon Mtn.
Aerial
Tramway

Cannon
Cliffs

93

Boise
Rock

P

RECREATIONAL TRAIL

3

P

**Franconia
Notch
State
Park**

Lafayette
Place East

Basin
West P

P Basin East

N

The Pool

Covered Bridge

The Flume

0   ½   1 MILE

P Flume
Visitor
Center

Hale

Old Man's Washbowl. The lake is well known for its brook trout and is open for fly fishing only.

Echo Lake

Beautiful Echo Lake, at an elevation of 1,931 feet, offers swimming, fishing and boating to park visitors, as well as views of Mount Lafayette and Cannon Mountain. In a different watershed from Profile Lake, its waters flow westerly toward the Connecticut River. Canoe and mountain bike rentals are available here.

Cannon Mountain Aerial Tramway

The first passenger aerial tramway in North America began operation on this site in 1938. Almost seven million passengers were carried to the top by the first tram. Tram II was completed in 1980, and today you can take a scenic five-minute ride in one of two enclosed cable cars to the 4,200-foot summit of Cannon Mountain and enjoy panoramic views of the distant valleys and mountains. Each tram has a car capacity of 80 people, and ascends 2,022 feet vertically over a horizontal distance of more than a mile.

Cannon is the home of the New England Ski Museum, which is located near the base of the tramway. It's open daily from 10-4, seasonally. Phone 603 823-5563.

Old Man of the Mountain
(The Great Stone Face Profile)

The Profile is a natural rock formation that was formed by a series of geologic happenings that began an estimated 200 million years ago. Hovering majestically 1,200 feet above Profile Lake, the Old Man is made of five separate granite ledges arrange horizontally to form a man's profile. From chin to forehead, the Profile measures about 40 feet and is 25 feet wide.

Look north a short distance from the Profile to see a natural rock formation silhouetted against the skyline resembling the barrel of a cannon poking out from the parapet of a fortress. The shape of this rock formation gives Cannon Mountain its name.

Franconia Notch State Parkway

Franconia Notch is one of New England's most spectacular slices of terrain with the towering peaks of the Franconia and Kinsman mountain ranges, and the steep slopes of Cannon Mountain to the west and Mount Lafayette's Eagle Cliffs to the east. Don't miss it.

Ride Information

Ride Level:	Beginner to intermediate. Great family riding.
Trail Distances:	As short as you want it to 21.2 miles out-and-back.
Trail Descriptions:	Smooth, paved road. Going south to north, a few gradual climbs.
Highlights:	See text. Basin, Flume Gorge, Profile Lake, etc., swimming, snack bars, gift shop, camping, picnic area, bird watching, fishing, photo ops.
Start:	Take I-93 north to Franconia Notch Parkway (after I-93 exit 33). Parkway exit 1 takes you to the Flume Visitor Center.
Note:	The park is open to bikers from thaw to first snow. Lift-served mountain biking is available at nearby Bretton Woods Ski Area, Loon Mountain and Waterville Valley.
	State highway maps are available free at state rest areas and many area businesses. Most sights are free. A fee is charged for such attractions as a tour of Flume Gorge or the Cannon Mountain aerial tramway.
	Bike rentals are available at Parkway exit 3, the Peabody Base Lodge.
	Brochures and maps of Franconia Notch State Park are available from the New Hampshire Division of Parks at 603 271-3556.
	Don't forget your bike lock in case you stop and explore.

Ride Options

1. Franconia Notch Recreation Path. From the Flume parking lot, take the recreation path heading north. The rec trail is well marked. This ride can be as short as you'd like. Just stop anywhere and return to the parking lot. But it can be as long as 21.2 miles round trip if you go to the northern terminus of the path that ends near Route 3.

The trail from south to north rises 1,000 vertical feet in a gradual climb, crossing several bridges and rolling along nicely. It crosses under Franconia Notch Parkway (which connects I-93 north and south of the notch) several times. This trail is even good in "bug season." The bugs are still there, but you can easily keep moving and stay ahead of them.

Along the way is the Basin. For a bracing swim, try Echo Lake. Snack bars and public rest rooms are available at Parkway exits 1, 2 and 3. The aerial tramway is open virtually all year at Cannon Mountain. The New England Ski Museum is open seven-days-a-week in the summer and offers free admission.

CHAPTER 6

BLACK MOUNTAIN STATE FOREST

Typical of New Hampshire, this area offers a little of everything. Rich dairylands of the Upper Connecticut Valley in the Haverhill area. Views of the craggy summits of the White Mountains. A slice of rural New England—the village of Benton, NH. A spectacular view in all directions from the top of Black Mountain.

The ride offers diversity, too. The Black Mountain State Forest area can satisfy the beginner, while at the same time present a real challenge to expert riders who choose to stray off onto the rutted abandoned woods roads like Black Mountain Trail (indicated in ride options 2 and 3). Three unimproved stream crossings are rideable in normal water levels. But when it's 90 degrees out and humid, who cares?

Climb Black Mountain if you want to add to your day's activities. This mountain top was the site of an old Forest Service fire tower.

The ride is basically a six-mile loop, about half is on Route 116, an infrequently traveled paved road leaving from downtown Benton. Nearby sight-seeing areas are mentioned below.

Franconia Notch State Park

A short drive to Franconia from here offers even more bicycling opportunities at Franconia State Park. The park, which has claimed national notoriety as one of the best in the U.S., offers a 22-mile bike path. Great for family entertainment. See previous chapter for details.

White Mountain National Forest Region

The 773,000-acre White Mountain National Forest with its rugged mountain peaks and rolling hills offers some of the best hiking, walking and biking trails anywhere. Over 1,300 miles of trails to choose from.

The forested areas are spectacular during foliage season. For some of the very best viewing, check out the Kancamagus Highway, the only National Scenic Byway in New England, it climbs to nearly 3,000 feet as it winds through the White Mountain National Forest from the Pemigewasset River in Lincoln to Conway.

Throughout the White Mountains are historic grand resort hotels, natural and family attractions. If this is a family outing, in addition to your bike ride, consider visiting the Conway Scenic Railroad in North Conway, visit Heritage where you can step back in time to 1634, or drive the Mt. Washington Auto Road to the top of the famous peak.

The Mt. Washington Valley comprises Conway, North Conway, Albany, Madison, Eaton, Bartlett, Intervale, Glen and Jackson. Besides its spectacular scenery, the Valley offers a wealth of lodging and dining choices, hiking, swimming and the largest collection of outlet stores in the state.

Farther north, on Route 16 from North Conway, you travel on to Jackson and the Jackson Covered Bridge, through Pinkham Notch and past a toll road that takes you to the summit of Mt. Washington. In Gorham you can take Route 2 east through the Shelburne birches area. The northern route (Route 16) leads you to Berlin, and provides access to the North Country.

Moose Capital of New Hampshire

The Northern White Mountains area of New Hampshire—over 3,000 square miles of rolling countryside and spectacular mountain scenery—is the moose capital of the state. From July 4th through foliage season moose tours are offered. Reservations are strongly suggested. Call the Northern White Mountains Chamber of Commerce at 800-992-7480 in Berlin, NH.

Lost River Gorge

Lost River Gorge was created long before recorded history, when glaciers ground their way across North America, shaping the land. To-

Black Mountain State Forest

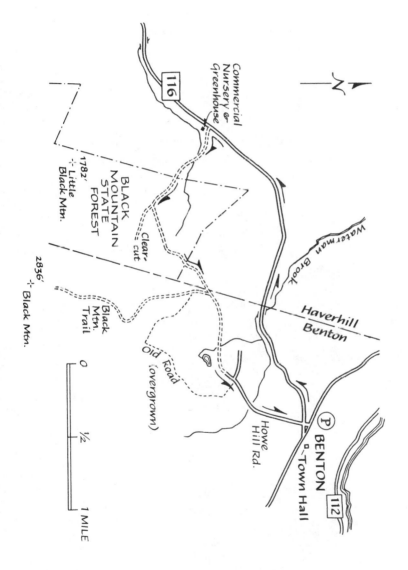

116

Commercial
Nursery &
Greenhouse

BLACK
MOUNTAIN
STATE
FOREST

Clear-
cut

1782'
Little
Black Mtn.

2836'
Black Mtn.

Black
Mtn.
Trail

Old Road
(overgrown)

Waterman Brook

Haverhill
Benton

Howe
Hill Rd.

P BENTON
Town Hall

112

0   ½   1 MILE

day you can follow Lost River as it appears and disappears through the narrow steep-walled gorge, the tumbled granite, crevasses, caverns and falls. The self-guided tour, which takes about an hour, teaches you about natural history, ecology and plant life. Children love to climb about the Hall of Ships, squeeze through the Lemon Squeezer and stand under Guillotine Rock. (All the caves can be by-passed for those of you who don't like enclosed spaces.) The site also offers a geological display and a nature garden with over 300 varieties of flowers, ferns and shrubs. Lost River is on Route 112, Kinsman Notch in North Woodstock. Call 603 745-8031.

Heritage-New Hampshire

This unique attraction uses life-size theatrical sets, state-of-the-art technology and period characters to bring New Hampshire's most fa-

Many kinds of wildlife, like this Great Blue Heron, call New Hampshire state forests home for the summer.

mous people and events to life. You travel through time from 1634 through 300 years. Visitors meet with early New England settlers and explore Portsmouth Town Square during the Revolution. Their newest attractions include a 120-foot-long historical mural, a glass silo and an old-fashioned trolley ride. In Glen, Heritage-New Hampshire is on Route 16. Call 603 383-9776.

For hundreds of other ideas, pick up a copy of *The Official New Hampshire Guidebook* at state information centers along I-93, write the New Hampshire Office of Travel and Tourism at Box 1856, Concord, NH 03302-1856, or call the New Hampshire Office of Travel and Tourism at 603 271-2343, to request a free copy.

Ride Information

Ride Level:	Beginner to expert. Experts, see options 2 and 3.
Trail Distances:	6-mile loop. Add Clear-cut spur (a half mile one way) and Black Mountain Trail (2.3 miles to top of Black Mountain) for expert riders.
Trail Descriptions:	Moderate riding. Gradual ascents/descents. Smooth, paved road for half of ride. Expert area has rutted back woods travel. Great views from atop Black Mountain, if you have the stamina to climb it!
Highlights:	Vistas of White Mountains. Quiet, deserted riding.
Start:	Take Route 10 to the village of North Haverhill, turn onto Route 116. Follow Route 116 to Benton, NH. Limited parking is available at Benton Town Hall, just east of the intersection.
Note:	The forest doesn't get much use except during hunting season, when it behooves you to avoid it or wear hunter orange.
	There is no charge to visit this forest. All trails on Black Mountain State Forest and the White Mountain National Forest land in this area are open to bikers. But stay on designated loops when on private land. Don't abuse the privilege, or we'll lose it.

Ride Options

1. Six-mile loop ride. For beginner and intermediate riders. From the Benton Town Hall, go west on Route 116 for 2.5 miles. Just before a commercial nursery and greenhouse, turn left on a gravel road. Wind past some seasonal camps and cross a branch of Clark's Brook on a crude wooden bridge at 2.8 miles. The road climbs steadily and crosses state forest boundary lines (painted blue). As you enter Black Mountain State Forest, you'll soon come to a Y in the road. Your odometer will read 3.2 miles. Stay left. (Experts: go right if you'd like—see ride option 2.)

The land flattens out. After a second stream crossing, a stand of red pines is on your right. A third stream crossing presents a challenge. It drops steeply into the streambed and climbs out on slick bedrock. Be careful. At 3.8 miles you cross another blue forest boundary area and leave state land. Please respect the private property you are entering. At 4.1 miles is an intersection with Black Mountain Trail. (Expert riders: see option 3.)

Follow the contour of the slope. The road surface improves. At 4.6 miles is the parking lot for Black Mountain Trail (hikers). The road surface is paved at 5.0 miles. The ride finishes with a screamer downhill on Howes Hill Road into Benton and your starting point.

2. Clear-cut Trail. (Expert) This is the same route as option 1 to 3.2 miles. Take the right fork at Y. It goes out half a mile. It climbs steeply uphill. At the end is a 20-acre clear-cut that was harvested in 1989 to regenerate paper birch.

3. Black Mountain Trail. (Expert) Follow option 1 for 4.1 miles. Take right on Black Mountain Trail. Masochists are welcome to continue on if the want to test their aerobic fitness. It ascends steeply!! for 2.3 miles to the top of Black Mountain. Elevation: 2,836 feet. Remember, the farther you go uphill, the more fun you will have on the downhill! For serious riders only.

CENTRAL REGION

CHAPTER 7

HEMENWAY STATE FOREST

Hemenway State Forest, a picturesque state forest which includes a natural area in Tamworth, is in the shadow of some of the most striking peaks of the White Mountain National Forest, most notably Mount Chocorua. The forest, in the northern Lakes region, also offers primo views of the Ossipee and Sandwich Ranges. On a clear day you can see into Maine.

Tamworth village, like many of the small towns in the Lakes region, retains its rural identity, as shown by its farmland, forests, church and New England architecture.

As in most New Hampshire forests, no park headquarters exist, but the area welcomes the public. A well-established network of trails, which are perfect for mountain biking, are maintained during the winter months by the Tamworth Outing Club, a local cross-country ski club. The club also installed trail map bulletin boards at the major trailheads, with trail maps available for a donation. (Although the racks tend to be empty in the summer. Use the one in this book instead.)

For nature lovers, Duck Pond offers a real treat. The pristine pond is a short ride off the main trail. There, you can observe several beaver families. The pond has a machine-made concrete dam that's barely visible and allows you to stand below water level, look across the surface of the pond and watch the antics of these busy water rodents.

Beavers in North America are recognized as natural conservationists. The dams they build help control the flow of mountain streams, preventing soil erosion and creating new homes for plants and animals. Today they are legally protected in most countries.

This area also shows evidence of the presence of moose, deer and bear. A fire tower at Great Hill offers spectacular views if you want to climb to the top.

The location of the forest should be a tip-off to the terrain you'll encounter. A variety of trails, from very rough single-track to wide-open gravel roads, lend themselves to the intermediate-level rider. There's very little flat riding, with some of the terrain being very steep and technical (i.e., logs across the trails, roots, rocks, blackberry brambles at perfect leg-tearing height.)

For other points of interest in the Lakes Region, see Chapter 11.

Ride Information

Ride Level: Intermediate to expert

Trail Distances: Vary. Loops can be as short as 3 miles to over 13 miles if you combine the loops.

Trail Descriptions: Steep at times. Sometimes gravel, sometimes double-track. Logs on trails in some areas.

Highlights: Several beaver families on Duck Pond. Quiet, deserted riding.

Start: From the Route 113/113A intersection in the center of Tamworth village, go north on Route 113A approximately 5 miles to the entrance of Hemenway State Forest. A large wooden sign announces you're in the right place. Go left on the gravel park road to a clearing on the left across from the trailhead intersection of Hemenway North and South End Trails. Bulletin board here.

Note: The forest shares trails with equestrians. (Watch out for land mines!) Always stop and allow the horse and rider to pass.
There is no charge to visit this forest. Don't stray onto private land. Remain only on marked trails.

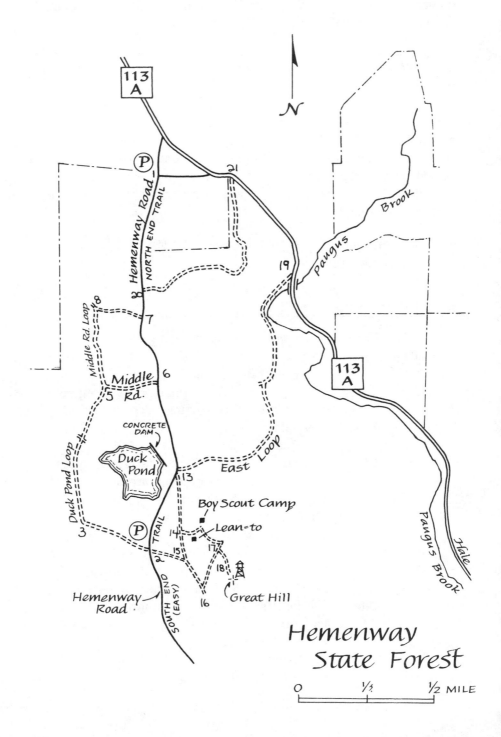

113
A

N

P

Hemenway Road

NORTH END TRAIL

21

Brook

Paugus

19

Middle Rd. Loop

8

7

113
A

Middle
Rd.

5

6

CONCRETE
DAM

Duck Pond Loop

4

Duck
Pond

East Loop

13

Boy Scout Camp

Lean-to

3

P

SOUTH END PT TRAIL

14

15

17

18

Great Hill

16

Hemenway
Road

SOUTH END
(EASY)

Paugus Brook

Hale

Hemenway
State Forest

0   ⅓   ½ MILE

Ride Options

To make this a little easier, we've inserted intersection numbers to take you from one point to another.

1. Hemenway Road North End Trail. (From intersection 1 to 2.) This is a smooth gravel road. Out-and-back is 3 miles. You'll encounter a half-mile climb before the intersection of Middle Road. Steep in sections.

2. Duck Pond Loop. A 2-mile loop from Hemenway Road. If you want to see the beaver families, you have to earn it. You start at intersection 6 to 2, 3, 5 and back to 6. This ride has really rough riding from intersection 2 to 3, then pricker bushes and slippery bogs. It's a very pretty section of the trail though, and section 3 to 5 isn't too challenging.

You'll come to an open field. Bear to the right, downhill through the center of the field. The trail re-enters the woods at the bottom of the field and is designated with red markers on the trees. The next section of trail (5 to 6), is up and down with some downed trees across the trail, so caution should be exercised. Soon you're back where you began at Hemenway Road.

3. Middle Road Loop. 1.5 mile loop. Starting at intersection 6 to 5, 8, 7 and back to 6. A short loop down Middle Road, then right on rolling double-track with deep tire ruts, some rocky sections with downed logs. It can be ridden as a fast, fun section by more experienced riders.

Turn right up a steep hill at intersection 8. As you near the bottom of this trail, there's a gate. Slow down to avoid being beheaded. You're back at Hemenway Road. Turn right to return to intersection 6 or left to go back to the parking area.

4. East Loop. 3.3-mile loop. Start at intersection 13 to 19, 1 and back to 13. Starting at the trailhead directly across from Duck Pond (you can see the pond through the trees), turn left on the trail and proceed through a small clearing following the trail markers designating the trail as used by equestrians. Give way to any horses on this trail.

This trail (13 to 19) is a 1.2-mile long downhill with some steeper sections that have water bars. The trail is a lot of fun, but you must keep your riding under control in case horses are also on the trail. Some sections have large puddles in the middle of the trail.

At the bottom of the trail you exit onto Route 113A. Turn left for .8 mile back to the park entrance. Turn left again on Hemenway Road and ride back to intersection 13 for a completed loop.

5. Great Hill Loop. This is a short loop. Starting at intersection 2 to 15, 16, 17, 18, back to 17, 14, 13 and back to 2. Starting at the bulletin board at the Hemenway Road South End Trail, follow the trail that goes uphill directly to the right of the bulletin board (2 to 15) for .1 mile of moderate gravel double-track. Bear right at the first trail junction and continue uphill on looser gravel. At intersection 16, take a sharp left and follow this grassy double-track up a rutted double-track steep climb that ends at the base of the fire tower on top of Great Hill. The view from the fire tower is fantastic! You can see Mt. Chocorua and Mt. Pasaconoway clearly when looking north, and Tamworth village when looking west/southwest.

Ride back down the tower access road (18 to 17) and bear right past an old, abandoned shack. Follow the trail downhill (steep in places), past a Boy Scout camp on your right and then Boy Scout lean-tos on the left, to the trail intersection at 14. This descent is technical in places, with deep ruts and very steep sections. At intersection 14, bear right gradually downhill until you drop back onto South End Trail. Take a left on South End Trail and you're back at the bulletin board after .3 mile of flat, smooth, gravel road.

6. Other Trails. The map has a lot of options. You could continue south beyond intersection 16, which links back to Hemenway. Hemenway Road also continues south beyond intersection 2. It's wide gravel surface with little traffic is nice for riding. You can also do the intersection 20 to 21 loop back to Route 113A. Or take on a challenge and do all of them!

CHAPTER 8

GILE STATE FOREST

Fat-tire heaven, to be sure, this neck of the woods in Springfield, New Hampshire! Just off a quiet stretch of Route 4A between Concord and Hanover, this maze of trails exists in Gile State Forest for all mountain bike levels. Choose from long, challenging loop rides to easy, roll-along gravel roads.

Gile State Forest trails and local town roads offers a fascinating network of trails that you probably can't accomplish in a day. But take the challenge and try it anyway.

Many of the trails in this forest are maintained by local snowmobile clubs, who've gained permission to pass onto private property—during the winter only. So—don't stray from the trails outlined in this guide or you may be trespassing and potentially ruining the privilege for others, as well as yourself in the future.

One of the roads, King's Highway, a double-track trail, was a main trail for New England settlers. Built in 1773, all that remains of the road of our long ago ancestors are a few cellar holes, stone walls and an overgrown wagon trail. Nowadays the transportation is in the form of snowmobiles and bicycles. Taking a left off the King's Highway can take you on a long, rocky challenging ride all the way to Little Sunapee Lake.

Ride Information

Ride Level:	Beginner to expert.
Trail Distances:	Vary. Loops can be as short as 3 miles to over 40+ miles if you cover all the trails.
Trail Descriptions:	Flat gravel to steep at times.
Highlights:	Huge network of choices. Fairly quiet and uninhabited. Visit Little Sunapee Lake. Nice view of Mt. Cardigan. Historic North Wilmot Church.
Start:	Gardner Memorial Wayside Park. To get there, take exit 11 off I-89 for 7 miles to Route 4A, just before a gas station. Turn left (north) on Route 4A for 7 miles to the park on right. A second starting point is in New London. See ride option 6 for directions.
Note:	There is no charge to visit this forest. Don't stray onto private land. Per usual, state forest boundaries are marked with blue paint. Also note this is a popular hunting destination during deer season, so avoid it then.

Ride Options

To make this a little easier, intersection numbers have been inserted to more easily take you from one point to another.

Note: Avoid these roads:

• **Butterfield Pond Trail** is very difficult, narrow and teeming with stumps and rocks.

• **Willow View Road** is impassable. Beavers have flooded the area.

1. Aaron Ledge Trail. Advanced ride. Approximately 7 miles out and back. To get there from parking area travel north to Route 4A (intersection 2). Then proceed to intersections 3, 12, 13. Turn left on the spur road to Aaron's Ledge, then back to 13, 12, 3, 2, 1. The short stretch of Fowler Town Road that you'll be on is quite challenging. You'll want to be aware of the blue state boundary markers. This trail eventually leaves the forest property and enters private property. Stay off private land.

2. Old Grafton Road Loop. From intersection 2, travel to 18, 17, 16, 15, 12, 3 and back to 2. This 12-mile loop, starting on Route 4A and Piper Pond Road finds fairly easy travel on Route 4A. It eventually gets

58

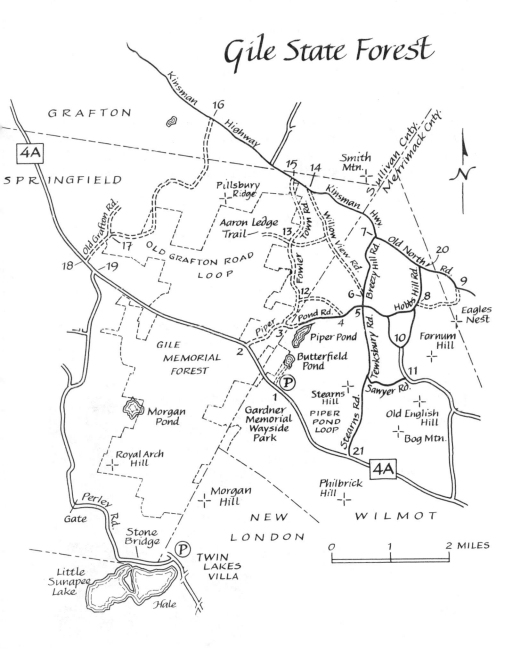

Gile State Forest

GRAFTON

Kinsman Highway 16

4A

SPRINGFIELD

Smith Mtn.

15 14

Sullivan Cnty.
Merrimack Cnty.

N

Pillsbury Ridge

Kinsman Hwy.

Aaron Ledge Trail

13

Willow View Rd.

7

Old North Rd.

20

Old Grafton Rd.

17

OLD GRAFTON ROAD LOOP

Fowler Town Rd.

Breezy Hill Rd.

9

18   19

12

7

6

Hobbs Hill Rd.

8

Eagles Nest

Piper   Pond Rd.

4

5

10

Farnum Hill

GILE MEMORIAL FOREST

2

3

Piper Pond

Tewksbury Rd.

11

Butterfield Pond

P

1

Stearns Hill

Sawyer Rd.

Old English Hill

Morgan Pond

Gardner Memorial Wayside Park

PIPER POND LOOP

Stearns Rd.

Bog Mtn.

Royal Arch Hill

Perley Rd.

Morgan Hill

21

Philbrick Hill

4A

WILMOT

Gate

Stone Bridge

NEW

LONDON

0   1   2 MILES

P

TWIN LAKES VILLA

Little Sunapee Lake

Hale

59

quite tricky on Fowler Town Road. So if you're a rookie, pick something else. A right on Old Grafton Road offers super mountain biking on this abandoned, little-used town road. You'll encounter several water bars and wooden bridges along the way to Kinsman Highway. Near where they intersect, gaze northward for an outstanding view of Mount Cardigan. At Kinsman Highway, turn right, and right again on Fowler Town Road. As you near the intersection with Piper Pond Road (13), you have half a mile of ledgy ruts to contend with.

3. North Wilmot Church Loop. Starting from the North Wilmot Church on Piper Pond Road at intersection 5, you can add an easy 4-mile loop to your ride. Intersection sequence is: 5, 7, 20, 8, and back to 5. The church, built in 1829, stands alone in the quiet woods, where nature creates her own form of worship.

4. Route 4A out and back. This ride is appropriate for a beginner rider. Route 4A is paved and has little traffic. Ride as far in either direction as you'd like.

5. Piper Pond Loop. Intermediate 8-mile ride. Intersection sequence: 1, 2, 3, 5, 21 and back to 1. Piper Pond Road is ledgy with steps to climb. Tewksbury Road is rougher still and takes you over larger hills, with a 1.5 mile descent to Stearns Road. Then return to Route 4A.

Ellen Chandler

A pause at Piper Pond—good moose territory!

6. Twin Lakes Villa Trail. This ride begins in New London (or you can get there by going out the King's Highway, taking a left on Perley Road). This ride is on all dirt roads, once you leave the paved road. Park at Cricenti's Market on Main Street (Old Route 11) or on the side of the road by the New London Town Beach.

Bike toward the Twin Lakes Villa Resort, go past the main "lodge," and just before a small stone bridge-dam, take a right up a dirt road. This is 1.7 miles from Cricenti's. The road is gated a quarter of a mile from the paved road. Although traveled by vehicles, this road gets little traffic. At .9-mile from the trailhead there's a fork.

Bear right up a steep hill. (Don't go left—it belongs to the water precinct and they'd rather not have visitors on their property.) As you finish this climb, you'll cross a large power line area that is cut wide and provides some nice vistas. After almost two miles, the road switches back to the left (north) and very soon you are at what has to be the most pristine mountain lake in central New Hampshire, Morgan Pond. The original water source for New London, the pond is the perfect place for a picnic, photos or even a nap. Just avoid the bug season!

Go on to Route 4A if you want to do a huge loop or turn back and retrace your tracks.

CHAPTER 9

WADE STATE FOREST

A quiet, undiscovered forest, Wade State Forest, in Hill, New Hampshire, is a mountain biker's jewel. Just north of Concord and close to two others sites mentioned in this book (Gile State Forest and Franklin Falls Reservoir), this getaway promises a fun day with lots of other interesting attractions nearby. You won't be greeted by a large sign or a forest ranger station. You won't find a well-stocked concession stand. Nor even a public beach. But you will find 463 acres of forest and town roads flanked by timeworn stone walls, sun dappling through the birch and hardwood trees, panoramic views of Mount Cardigan (especially during foliage season), and even a small cemetery with a dozen headstones dating back to the mid-1800s. And the soul-healing sounds of Smith River as it careens off the ledges in early spring. If you're so inclined, Smith River, a tributary of the Pemigewasset, offers great trout fishing. It's just a mile away. And if you're an early riser, you might even catch a glimpse of deer grazing. Wade State Forest is worth the drive from anywhere.

The trails are appropriate for the beginner to intermediate. If you stay on the maintained town gravel roads, you'll have a nice network of options to explore and a basically flat ride with some rolling ascents. If you can or want to handle more of a challenge, take on Center Trail. It's rocky in places, there are several streams to cross and the trail is a bit undefined at times. Fortunately there are neon green paint markers sprayed on trees periodically to give you direction.

Wade State Forest is 35 miles north of Concord, New Hampshire's capital city. Following are some historical and interesting attractions in the capital region that you may wish to check out as part of your biking vacation or day trip.

Capital Region

Concord began as a small trading post in 1659 along the Merrimack River. Nearby is Penny Cook (later to be called Penacook), a bend in the river where in 1697 pioneer woman Hannah Duston escaped from Indian captors, scalped them while they slept and escaped. This site is recognized with a memorial near exit 17 off I-93. It's on the left as you travel west toward Franklin and Hill.

Concord is the state capital and home of the world-famous Concord Coach. You can see a beautifully restored coach at the New Hampshire Historical Society in Concord. A marvel of coach engineering, each one weighed about 2,400 pounds and cost between $777 and $1,250. About 3,000 coaches in 40 styles were created by a Concord wheelwright and a journeyman coach builder. They opened up the West and put Concord, NH on the map.

Also within easy walking or driving distance of the Capitol Building and State House are historic Kimball-Jenkins Estate, The Rev. Timothy Walker House and Daniel Webster's birth place in West Franklin. Other points of interest in the Concord area:

The Pierce Manse

Franklin Pierce lived in this Concord home from 1842 to 1846, before his election in 1852 as 14th President of the United States. Much of the family's furniture, furnishings and tableware is still here.

Shaker Village

A definite "must see." Canterbury Shaker Village, a cluster of 22 buildings that celebrates life during a different era, is seven miles north of Concord. Located in a pristine and very picturesque setting of rolling hills and open fields, the village is maintained as a historical sight. The religious sect who "devoted its hands to work and hearts to God" was noted for being ahead of its time. It exhibited an egalitarian attitude toward work and education. All tasks, from washing clothes in their innovative washing and drying buildings to working the fields, were rotated so that everyone was equally skilled. The Shakers gladly took in

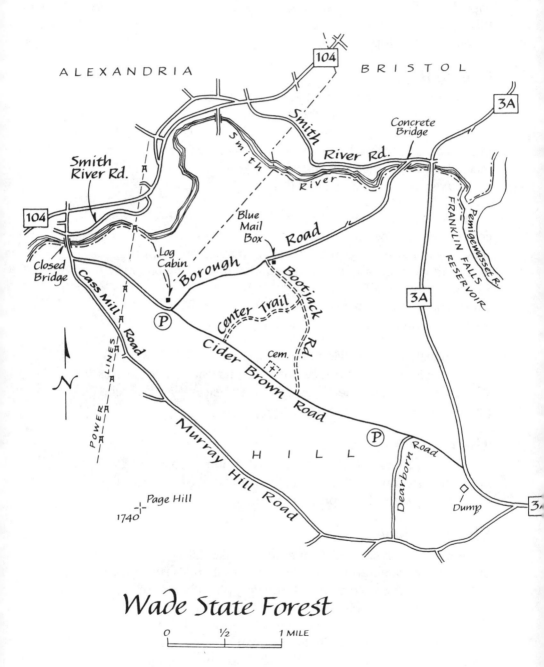

Wade State Forest

0   ½   1 MILE

orphans and taught and nurtured them to adulthood when they had the choice to stay in the village or go into the secular world.

Shakers invented many items that were innovative in their day. Clothes pins. Brooms. Simple ladder back caned chairs. High quality, very long-lasting paint. They initiated a mail order catalog for seeds. They also marketed herbs and medicines and of course, the famous Shaker boxes. The Shakers were also known for their delicious food. Stop by the Shaker museum, take a tour, check out their exceptional crafts in the shop, have a meal or snack in The Creamery Restaurant. But most of all, absorb the serenity.

Christa McAuliffe Planetarium

Concord high school teacher Christa McAuliffe hoped to use outer space as a classroom to stretch the imaginations of children. The hope was shattered with the explosion of the space shuttle Challenger in January of 1986. Christa had been chosen from among 11,000 teachers to be the first teacher-in-space. Her dream lives on in the planetarium named after her. This high-tech facility with its 40-foot dome provides an opportunity to abandon gravity and take part in a visual adventure, where a seat in the planetarium will hurtle you into space with high-speed simulation in 3D.

Ride Information

Ride Level:	Beginner to intermediate.
Trail Distances:	Vary. 5-mile loop or can be extended with adjacent roads and riding under power lines.
Trail Descriptions:	Basically flat, rolling ascent. Town-maintained gravel roads. Or choose trails that are rocky, have wet areas and are somewhat indistinguishable at times. Can do some riding on paved roads with little traffic.
Highlights:	Quiet. Lots of attractive scenery. Nice view of Mt. Cardigan. Near Concord and other points of interest.
Start:	Take I-93 north to exit 20. Take Route 3 and 11 west. Follow Route 11 to Route 3A. Take Route 3A north through Franklin to Hill. Go through Hill. On left you'll see Murray Hill Road. Continue on 3A half a mile. Just past the dump you'll see a gravel

road. It's Dearborn Road, but it's unmarked. Take
your next right on Cider Brown Road. Park along
the side of the road. Another parking area is about
a mile down Cider Brown Road across from a log
cabin. Please park out of the way.

Note: There is no charge to visit this forest.

Ride Options

1. Burrough Road Loop. Intermediate level 5-mile ride. Beginning at
the parking area closest to Route 3A on Cider Brown Road, head toward the other parking area. A half mile down on the right is Bootjack
Road. It's a wide road that has a stone wall on both sides. Basically flat
with rolling ascents. Great scenery here during foliage season especially. Panoramic views. Bootjack goes for about 1.5 miles and intersects with Burrough Road at a T. Turn left on Burrough Road. Landmark: a blue mail box is at this T. (Burrough Road is a town-maintained
gravel road, so watch out for traffic.) Follow Burrough Road to the next
T intersection. A log cabin is on your right. Take a left here on Cider
Brown Road. You'll contend with some rocks, roots and leaves on this
trail. Then you'll encounter a challenging uphill and cross over a stream.

2. Center Trail. If you are a strong intermediate rider, you might want
to add Center Trail to the ride above. It has a lot of brush and is quite
overgrown in places. You have to cross a stream—best to walk your
bike. It'll add a little over a mile one-way.

There are lots of deer on this trail, so keep an eye peeled. Also you
may encounter horses and riders. Give way to them. The trail becomes
indistinguishable at times now. Follow the neon green markings on the
trees.

As you near the end of Center Trail (Cider Brown Road end), there
are a couple of abandoned colonial cellarholes. The local lore says the
L-shaped hole constructed from granite field stone is the former home
owned by George Washington's bodyguard.

3. Cider Brown Road. Out and back it's a little over 6 miles. Super
beginner trail. This is a nice, wide gravel road. Some vehicle traffic.
Head away from Route 3A toward the parking area at the other end,

and keep going. You'll come to a T intersection with Burrough Road. Stay left on Burrough Road. Keep going and you'll pass under the power lines. You'll come to a T, turn right on Cass Mill Road and travel a short way. You'll be at a closed bridge. You can get to the other side by backtracking and traveling out Smith River Road.

4. Smith River Road. Beginner ride. From the parking area on Cider Brown Road, go toward Route 3A and take a left on 3A (paved) for 2.4 miles to Smith River Road. It's paved when you first turn on it. Turn left on Smith River Road. Turn left on Smith River Road. Go .3 mile to a cement bridge over the river on your left. Steep ledges on both sides channel the water. A soothing sight and sound. Take the left over the bridge. This is Burrough Road. Follow Burrough Road all the way to the T-intersection at Cass Mill Road. Take a right on Cass Mill Road to encounter the closed bridge.

5. Power Lines. Another option is to ride under the power lines. From the second parking area, pick up Cass Mill Road. It's a paved road that seems like an extension of Cider Brown Road. Two-tenths of a mile or so up are the power lines. The paths along here tend to be smooth and provide good views as the vegetation is kept back from the lines.

CHAPTER 10

HEATH POND BOG NATURAL AREA

Heath Pond Bog is what's known in geological circles as a kettle bog. A kettle bog is a depression left in a mass of glacial drift, formed by the melting of an isolated block of glacial ice. This natural area in Ossipee, in New Hampshire's Lakes Region, covers over 1,300-square acres, but due to the nature of a bog, it's mostly wetlands. So even though the biking might not be as extensive as some areas, it has other unique features—like thriving wetlands, where if you're patient and quiet, you can photograph waterfowl, Great Blue Herons and moose. Features like a feverish beaver colony that offers great opportunities for viewing nature at work. Heath Pond, where much of the activity occurs, is accessible by footpath—a short walk and you're there.

The area is near a couple of others mentioned in the book, should you want to combine them. Heath Pond Bog is near Hemenway State Forest and Pine River State Forest. The roads are packed sand and very flat. Good for a leisure ride or family nature outing.

For other points of interest in the Lakes Region, see Chapter 11.

Ride Information

Ride Level: Beginner to intermediate.
Trail Distances: Vary. If you ride all the trails, loops and spur roads on map, it would be maybe 3 miles.
Trail Descriptions: Basically flat. Packed sand.
Highlights: Quiet. Nature lovers haven. Beaver colony.

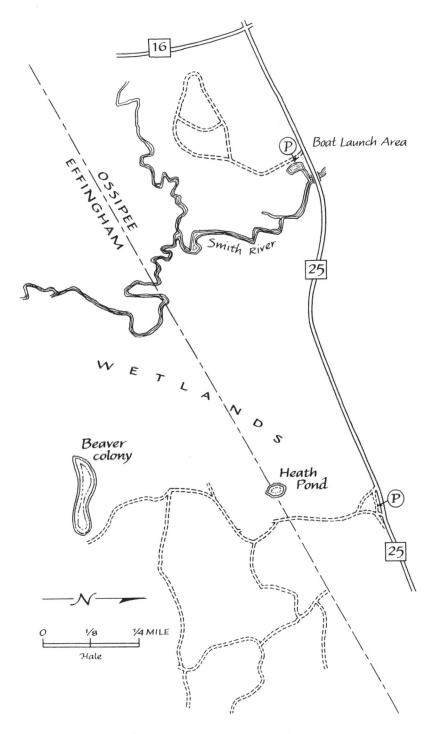

16

Boat Launch Area

P

OSSIPEE
EFFINGHAM

Smith River

25

W E T L A N D S

Beaver
colony

Heath
Pond

P

25

N

0   ⅛   ¼ MILE

Hale

Heath Pond Bog Natural Area

Start: From Routes 16/25 in Ossipee, take Route 25 northeast nearly 2 miles to Heath Pond Bog (or only go 1 mile to the boat launch area and docking facilities). Both places have parking, with rides starting from both areas. (You can ride the mile in between on your bike or drive down.)

Note: There is no charge to visit this natural area. Please ride on the trails outlined on the map and respect the privacy of land owners that adjoin the property.

Ride Options

1. Boat Launch Area. Intermediate level 5-mile ride. This area, about a mile from the Route 16/25 intersection (going northeast on Route 25), has a small network of trails to explore. Check them out, then ride down Route 25 to the Heath Pond Bog trails.

2. Heath Pond Bog Trails. Two miles northeast on Route 25 from the Route 16 intersection, you'll come to Heath Pond Bog Natural Area. A plaque explaining kettle bogs assures you you're at the right spot. Scout around on the network of trails on this end. Quite a bit of logging has been done in this area over the years, so many logging skid roads and landings exist. Avoid the road to the left a third of a mile before the beaver pond unless you're ready for a more rugged ride. If you do stay with it, you can complete a loop and end up back by Heath Pond.

CHAPTER 11

PINE RIVER STATE FOREST

"This is a mountain biker's paradise, but nobody knows about it." That's what the New Hampshire state forester for this region says about Pine River State Forest in the Effingham-Ossipee area of the Lakes Region. He's not trying to keep it a secret, but is only saying that this area is spectacular for biking, and very few people are aware of it. But now you know. It's perfect—over 50 miles of roads and trails, pretty scenery, a picnic area, sightings of moose, deer, black bear, coyote, fox, various birds (grouse, partridge, redtail hawks, broadwing hawks, song birds), even a couple of beaver colonies. And miles to go before you sleep.

This forest is in the center of the state, in the northern area of the Lakes Region, a favorite among vacationers and natives alike. The richness in diversity is a taste of Utopia. A scattering of 273 lakes and ponds set against a backdrop of rolling hills and stately mountains. If you want to get in some hiking while you're up here biking, check out Rattlesnake Mountain or Abenaki Tower off Route 109 in Melvin Village. Historic New England villages abound—there's Wolfeboro and Sandwich. Belknap Mill, a year-round center for the arts in the oldest unaltered brick textile mill in America, is worth a visit.

The Lakes Region of New Hampshire covers a lot of ground—from Rochester on the Seacoast, to Franklin and Bristol on the western border, Plymouth and Tamworth in the north. Other points of interest in the Lakes Region of New Hampshire:

Pine River State Forest

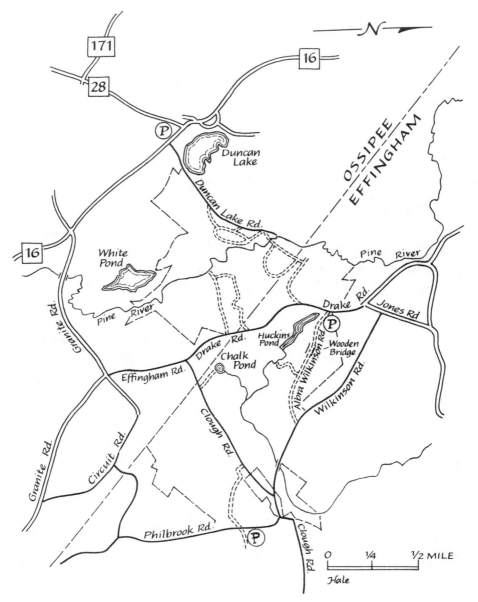

On Golden Pond

All you Katharine Hepburn and Henry Fonda fans from the film *"On Golden Pond,"* here's your opportunity to take a boat tour on the actual pond where the movie was filmed. You might even hear the loons who call this area home. For information, call 603 279-4405, the Original Golden Pond Tour Company or Squam Lake Tours at 603 968-7577.

The Science Center of New Hampshire

Located near the shores of Squam Lake, the Science Center offers the opportunity to wander through a 200-acre wildlife sanctuary. The trail features native New Hampshire animals—black bear, whitetail deer, owls, foxes, eagles, hawks, otters and the stately bald eagle—in natural settings. The Center, which also has a picnic area and nature store, is on Route 113 in Holderness. Call 603 968-7194.

Polar Caves Park

This park has been a family adventure destination since 1922. You can explore the caves on a self-guided tour and enjoy the woodland setting for a couple of hours or the entire day. There's also a Maple Sugar Museum, two gift shops, a snack bar, picnic area, ice cream shop and wildlife exhibits. Polar Caves Park is on Route 25 in Plymouth, 603 356-1888.

M/S Mount Washington

A visit to the Lakes Region is hardly complete without a cruise on the M/S Mount Washington. Take a 50-mile, three-hour cruise on Lake Winnipesaukee. The cruise ship has a full-service cafeteria, lounge and gift shop. During the summer enjoy a moonlight dinner/dance cruise. The cruise ship is docked on Route 3 in Weirs Beach, 603 366-BOAT.

That's a smattering of hundreds of opportunities to consider when in the Lakes Region. For a complete rundown, call the New Hampshire Department of Resources and Economic Development at 603 271-2666. They'll send you a free 200-page copy of *The Official New Hampshire Guidebook.* Or write for it at P.O. Box 1856, Concord, NH 03302-1856.

Ride Information

Ride Level:	Beginner to intermediate.
Trail Distances:	Vary. Numerous loops. 6.5+ miles.
Trail Descriptions:	Town-maintained roads, shared with very little car traffic. Trails are well-defined. Some steep areas, mostly flat or rolling.
Highlights:	Nature lovers haven. Two beaver colonies.
Start:	Travel north on Route 16. In Ossipee, take a right opposite Route 175. Go 1.7 miles to a 4-way intersection. Go left on Effingham Road (it becomes Drake Road). 2.5 miles from 4-way intersection is Huckins Pond. There's a dam here. Park alongside the road or in the small parking area on the south side of the dam. The maps offers 2 other parking areas.
Note:	There is no charge to visit this forest.

Ride Options

So many ride options exist, I'm not sure where to begin. I'll suggest a few, but the network is so big, you can come up with 16 others without effort. Just keep the map at hand.

1. Huckins Pond Loop. Beginner to intermediate ride. This 6.5-mile loop begins on Drake Road at one of the parking areas along a gravel town road. Continue traveling north on Drake Road a half a mile. Take a right turn. Shortly after that (about a quarter mile) turn right again, on Wilkinson Road. Go about 2.5 miles, and turn right on Clough Road. (You'll see several trails off Clough Road on your right. Take them if you'd like.) At T, take a right back on Drake Road and back to your car.

2. Addendum to Huckins Pond Loop. Fabulous trails exist inside the above loop. Near the dam where you parked your car at Huckins Pond, you'll see a trail that leads inside the loop. It's called Albra Wilkinson Road on the map. You'll soon be delighted as you come across a 48-foot-long wooden foot bridge. There are a number of spurs off this road. Check them out if you want.

3. Philbrook Loop. This beginner 7-mile loop starts from the parking area on Philbrook Road. It's a large area with several boulders. (There's also a trail that leads from the parking area over to Clough Road.) Go back out on Philbrook Road, take a left on Philbrook toward Clough Road. Left on Clough Road. Just before you intersect with Effingham Road there's a path on the right that's .2 mile long that leads to Chalk Pond. A beaver colony is located here. It's also a super place for a picnic. Remember carry out what you carried in.

Left on Effingham. Left on Circuit Road. Soon you intersect with Philbrook again. Take a left and soon you'll be back at the parking lot.

4. Duncan Lake Trails. This is an advanced beginner ride. Only because at times the trails are steep and rocky. But you can walk your bike over these areas. The steep, rocky areas are few. Of course, if you're doing an "out-and-back," you'll have as much "up as down."

You can start this ride from Huckins Pond or from the Duncan Lake parking area. The trails meet up. We'll take it from the Huckins Pond parking area.

Ride half a mile from the parking lot toward Effingham Road (south). On the right will be an unmarked snowmobile trail. Turn right on it. A short way in you'll come to a fork. If you go right for quite a ways, you'll arrive at Pine River. A beaver bog is in the distance to your right.

If you take the left turn back at the fork, it leads into a maze of other trails. Use the map to navigate around on them. I'd recommend going over to Duncan Lake Road where you'll be up on a ridge with nice views. To get there you'll cross a long wooden bridge.

CHAPTER 12

FRANKLIN FALLS RESERVOIR

This ride is so flat you may be bored. (I heard that yelp of triumph in the background!) If you're a beginner and love the flat ground, or if you are planning a family day with picnicking, swimming and mountain biking, or if you just want a long, flat run, this is it.

The Franklin Falls Flood Control Reservoir is maintained by the U.S. Army Corps of Engineers and is located north of Concord, overlapping the towns of Franklin and Hill. The reservoir is a super find if you're a mountain biker. This 6.5-mile (13 round-trip) ride is delightful. It offers miles and miles of quiet riding on old Route 3A. At the north end of the ride is Profile Falls, a cascading soul-soother that's a short walk from the parking area. Swimming is permitted. So pack a picnic lunch, go for a swim and fly down the trails on your bike to dry off. Just one note: this area has quite a bit of poison ivy. So beware!

This riding area is near Wade State Forest, which has a network of trails also. If you exhaust the Franklin Falls trails, drive down the road to the Wade State Forest trails. (See Chapter 9.) It's also a short drive to the State Forest Nursery and Mt. Kearsarge. They, too, have some good rides. (See Chapters 13 and 15.)

You are near Concord and the Capital Region of the state. If you want further suggestions of points of interest, Chapter 9 has that, too.

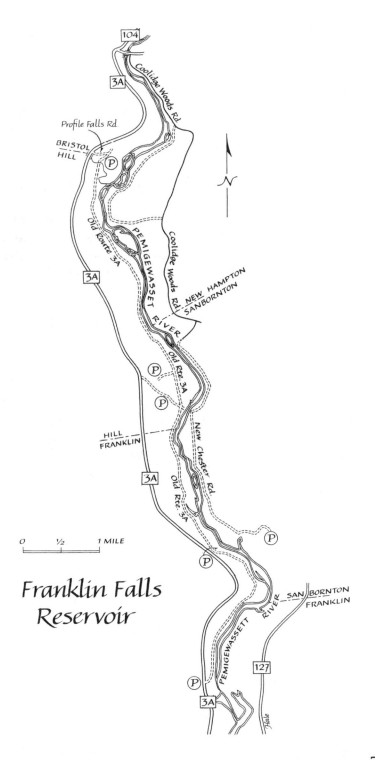

104

3A

Coolidge Woods Rd

Profile Falls Rd.

BRISTOL
HILL

P

Old Route 3A

PEMIGEWASSET RIVER

Coolidge Woods Rd.

NEW HAMPTON
SANBORNTON

3A

P

Old Rte. 3A

P

HILL
FRANKLIN

3A

New Chester Rd.

Old Rte. 3A

P

P

P

PEMIGEWASSETT RIVER

SANBORNTON
FRANKLIN

127

3A

Hale

O   ½   1 MILE

Franklin Falls
Reservoir

77

Ride Information

Ride Level: Beginner to intermediate.

Trail Distances: 13 miles round trip (out-and-back).

Trail Descriptions: Gravel roads, some tar roads and dirt trails.

Highlights: Profile Falls. Swimming. Picnic area. Near Concord attractions.

Start: Several parking areas to choose from. South entrance is 3 miles south of the Village Store in Hill Village on Route 3A. There's a log cabin at this entrance on right.

The north entrance is 4.3 miles north of Hill Village on Route 3A. On left is Smith River Road. On right is Profile Falls Road. Turn right on Profile Falls Road to T. Go right at T. Profile Falls parking here. Porta-potty here, too.

Note: There is no charge to visit Franklin Falls Reservoir.

Ride Options

1. Franklin Falls Reservoir. This is a 13-mile round trip beginner to intermediate ride. You can begin at either end or in the middle. A large network of trails guarantees to stave off boredom—even if it is flat. If 13 miles are too many, start at the north end by Profile Falls and take a shorter out-and-back route. Then come back and have a picnic and go swimming.

CHAPTER 13

STATE FOREST NURSERY

A state forest nursery? Did you know one existed? And did you know you can ride your mountain bike on the property? Me neither! But it's true and everybody benefits.

This ride offers nice mountain biking trails with a couple of waterfalls, a swimming pond and picnic area, and a chance to learn something about forests in New Hampshire. The roads and trails are appropriate for beginner and intermediate. They can be a bit challenging if you take some of the spur roads.

The trails all leave from the State Forest Nursery Complex. Foresters are usually around to answer questions. You ride on a trail past seed beds of white spruce, blue spruce and other young trees that are cultivated for sale on the state property. The tiny trees create a miniature forest. Consumers can purchase any variety of trees they desire—white pine, red pine, Norway spruce, Douglas fir, Scotch pine, Japanese Barberry, Bayberry—and even songbird or wildlife "packages."

Since the State Forest Nursery began in 1910, millions of tree and shrub seedlings have been distributed throughout the state. If you're interested in purchasing some seedlings, contact the Division of Forests and Lands at Box 1856, Concord, NH 03302-1856 or your county forester's office. Conifers are usually sold in multiples of 25, some require an order of 100, and deciduous trees in multiples of 25.

This trail area is about 17 miles from Wade State Forest, Franklin Falls Reservoir, and Blackwater Reservoir, which all have a network of mountain bike trails also. Check them out in Chapter 9, Chapter 12, and Chapter 14, respectively.

You are near Concord and the Capital Region of the state. If you want further suggestions of points of interest, Chapter 9 has that, too.

Ride Information

Ride Level:	Beginner to intermediate.
Trail Distances:	6 miles round trip if you ride Stirrup Iron Road. If you add Nursery Falls Trail and a couple of spur roads, you'll increase your mileage by a little over 4 miles.
Trail Descriptions:	Gravel town road with little car traffic. Trails are single-track, pine-needle covered paths. A half dozen puddles. Some uphill climbs.
Highlights:	A couple of sets of falls. One you have to really look for, but it's worth it. It has 25-foot drop-off ledges. Picnic spot. Swimming. Forest nursery is educational. Near Concord attractions.
Start:	Park near the State Forest Nursery equipment barns on the left. To get there, travel north on Route 3N through Boscawen. The nursery is 3.8 miles north on the left.
Note:	There is no charge to visit the State Forest Nursery. Please stay on trails designated on the map. The area surrounding the nursery is private property.

Ride Options

1. Stirrup Iron Road. Out-and-back is a 6-mile round trip. Beginner level. This is a town gravel road. Wide and in good shape. Occasional traffic passes. Leave the nursery parking lot and take a left on Route 3A for .2-mile to Stirrup Iron Road. Take a left. You can travel all the way to Route 127 on this gravel road. Return as you came.

At 1.2 miles up Stirrup Iron Road on the left is a small waterfall and swimming pond.

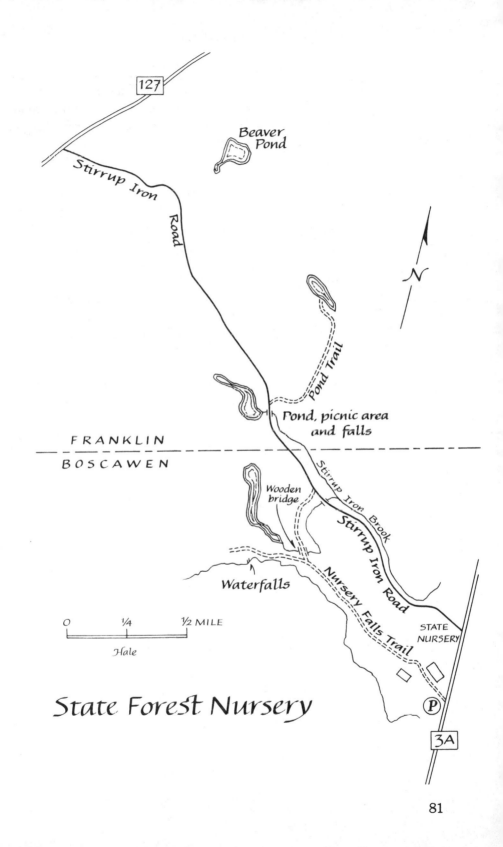

127

Beaver
Pond

Stirrup Iron

Road

N

Pond Trail

Pond, picnic area
and falls

FRANKLIN

BOSCAWEN

Wooden
bridge

Stirrup Iron Brook

Stirrup Iron Road

Waterfalls

Nursery Falls Trail

STATE
NURSERY

0   ¼   ½ MILE

Hale

P

State Forest Nursery

3A

81

2. Pond Trail. If you want a bit more rugged cycling, travel 1.2 miles down Stirrup Iron Road and take a right on Pond Trail. This is tricky to find, but once you do, you'll recognize it as there's a bit of clearing after you get on the trail. From here, you can travel .6-mile to a pond. To get there you trek over a half-dozen puddles, climb gradually for a third of a mile and descend to the pond. This is a popular snowmobile route.

3. Nursery Falls Trail. Probably more intermediate level ride. Unless you don't mind a short, steep ascent. But think about it. At the end, with a little perseverance, you'll find a waterfall embraced by a 25-foot drop-off and surrounded by hemlock trees. Perfect for a picnic.

To get there, travel up Nursery Falls Trail. At the fork where there's a wooden bridge down the way, take a left. On the left at the top of the hill, begin looking for a hatch mark about 7-feet off the ground on a tree. Walk down over the ridge to the waterfall. Follow the sound. Leave your bike—it'll be pretty impossible to bring it. It's too overgrown.

You can follow this trail a bit farther out—it terminates at some rocks where there's an old campfire clearing. Fires are not permitted.

If you go back to the fork in the road and go over the bridge, you can travel through to the gravel road, Stirrup Iron Road.

CHAPTER 14

BLACKWATER RESERVOIR

F lat. Flat. Flat. This area is *very* flat for the most part. You'll find a few inclines, but not many on this state-maintained, but U.S. Army Corps of Engineers-owned property called Blackwater Reservoir, in Webster and Salisbury, NH. With over 3,600 acres, this scenic flood control area teeming with wildlife and picture-pretty views of Mt. Kearsarge, Pat's Peak and Mt. Sunapee, is fabulous for mountain biking. With a soul-calming background of white pine, hemlock and birch interspersed, it's a perfect excuse to get the world in more balanced perspective. If you do all the trails, you could add more than 50 miles to your odometer. But if you'd rather just enjoy nature and have a picnic, spy on a beaver colony or go for a swim, you can do that, too.

The majority of these trails are snowmobile paths in the winter. During the summer, however, that means you have to cross streams when they are not frozen, so be prepared to do some wading or avoid the areas.

You are near Concord and the Capital Region of the state. If you want some suggestions of other activities or points of interest, check out Chapter 9.

Ride Information

Ride Level: Beginner to intermediate.
Trail Distances: Choose as long a ride as you'd like. If you do all the trails and roads, it will be more than 50 miles.

Trail Descriptions: Some packed gravel town roads with little car traffic. Trails are shaded, pine-needle covered. Some paved roads.

Highlights: Lots of wildlife. Beaver colony. This is a deer wintering yard. Good swimming holes and picnic area on Chairfactory Road along the river. Near Concord attractions.

Start: Park at the dam site. To get there, take 127 to Webster. Soon you'll see signs for Blackwater Dam. Park in the large lot. Or go left on Little Hill Road to Warner Road in Salisbury. Take a right. You'll see a yellow gate and a parking area.

Note: There is no charge to visit the reservoir. Roads may be blocked due to controlled flooding. Please stay on trails designated on the map. The surrounding area is private property.

Ride Options

To more easily identify turns, some intersections have been numbered on the map.

FYI: Cogswell Wood Road. If you're on Cogswell Wood Road and want to cross the river, do so where the trail is closest to the river. See the map. Ford the river here and do a loop to right and go back to the dam. You'll want to cross over at intersection 12 where it's shallow, because it is overgrown with vegetation farther down. In this area you'll see open fields by a stone wall—fabulous environment for wildlife. Keep an eye out.

1. Warner Road Loop. This is an 11.5-mile loop. You will probably encounter some puddles on this tour. From the Blackwater Dam parking lot, take Little Hill Road north. It begins as a paved road and becomes gravel as you glide downhill toward Warner Road. There are some pretty farms along the way. Also there's a beaver dam along this road. It was begun the summer of 1995. At intersection 2, take a right on Warner Road. You'll travel a short way and see the other parking area. You'll intersect with Route 127 (paved) at intersection 4. Go right on Route 127 back to the dam.

Blackwater Reservoir

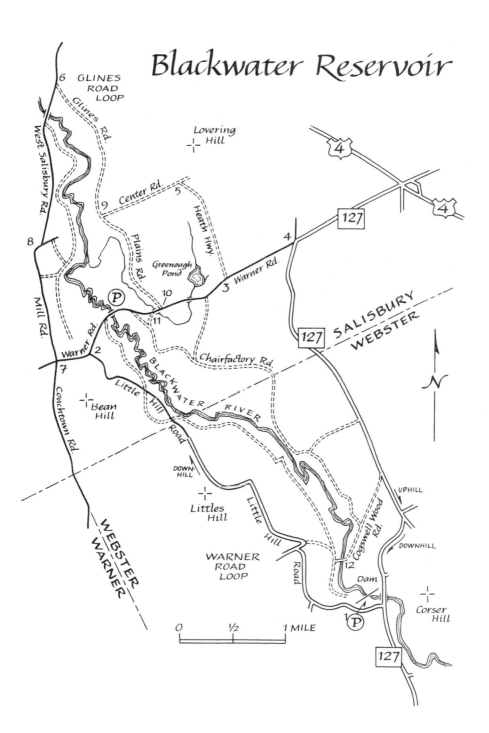

6 GLINES ROAD LOOP

Lovering Hill

West Salisbury Rd.

Glines Rd.

9 Center Rd. 5

Heath Hwy.

Plains Rd.

Greenough Pond

3 Warner Rd. 4

127

4

SALISBURY
WEBSTER

127

8

Mill Rd.

P

10

11

Warner Rd.

2

7

Chairfactory Rd.

BLACKWATER RIVER

N

Conchtown Rd.

Bean Hill

Little Hill Road

DOWN-HILL

Littles Hill

Little Hill Road

WARNER ROAD LOOP

Cogswell Wood Rd.

UPHILL

DOWNHILL

12

Dam

WEBSTER
WARNER

0   ½   1 MILE

P

Corser Hill

127

2. Glines Road Loop. This is really fun—19.5 miles of mountain bike challenge! Leave the dam site on Little Hill Road to intersection 2. Turn left to intersection 7. At intersection 7, go right on Mill Road. At Intersection 8, go right and then left on West Salisbury Road. At intersection 6 go right on Glines Road. At intersection 9, continue straight on Plains Road (a double track trail) to intersection 10 with Warner Road. Plains Road features spectacular views of Mt. Kearsarge. Take a right for a short distance. At the fork at intersection 11, go left on Chairfactory Road. Along Chairfactory are good swimming holes and picnic spots. Follow it along the river and you'll soon find yourself back at the dam where you began.

3. Other Options. They're really innumerable. Just take off and explore. Keep this map nearby so you don't get lost. Check out Heath Highway, Plains Road and Province Road. There are gizillions of town roads (gravel roads maintained by towns) with little vehicular traffic in this area (but not on the map) that are also super for biking. If you want to move beyond the boundaries of the map and cruise those roads, go for it!

CHAPTER 15

ROLLINS AND WINSLOW STATE PARKS

$\mathbf{N}$ow *this* is a real challenge—mountain biking up a mountain! Just kidding. You'll be cycling on roads around one of the oldest mountains in the state, Mt. Kearsarge, but they are flat! Located in Warner and Wilmot, Mt. Kearsarge is home of both Winslow and Rollins State Parks. Because of its easy accessibility to the parks, and outstanding summit vistas, Mt. Kearsarge, elevation 2,937 feet, is a popular family hiking destination. Views include nearby Sunapee, Ragged and Cardigan mountains and more distant Mt. Monadnock and Ascutney. On very clear days views extend to the White Mountains, the Green Mountains of Vermont, the Atlantic Ocean and Boston!

The exposed granite summit is a good place to see evidence of past glacial activity. During the glacial period more than 25,000 years ago, a great ice sheet more than a mile thick moved over Kearsarge and much of New Hampshire. Glacial striations, grooves cut in rock by the movement of glacial ice, can be seen on the summit, as well as on ledge outcroppings in the Winslow picnic area. Kearsarge's "bald head" summit is the result of a 1796 forest fire which burned the vegetation and exposed the soil to wind and water erosion.

A 3.5-mile winding paved toll road snakes its way up Mt. Kearsarge to the summit. The best way to enjoy this area is to plan to do a little mountain biking, hiking, picnicking and photography. On the way up this road are many turnouts for viewing and photos. (You'll want to walk the road, not ride it. Trails for mountain biking follow.) Half a mile from the summit is a picnic area. The summit has a fire tower. In the fall, migrating hawks are often seen from this vantage point. Also extremely popular, but a bit more colorful than the hawks, are hang-gliders, who launch themselves off the mountain toward the parking area far below.

Nearby is Winslow State Park, the other state park on Mt. Kearsarge. You go there on the mountain bike trails. The park is named in honor of John A. Winslow, a Union admiral during the Civil War. In 1864 Admiral Winslow, commander of the sloop *Kearsarge*, sank the Confederate gunboat *Alabama* during a decisive battle.

The auto road climbs to the 1,820-foot level of the 2,937-foot mountain. There, you'll find a picnic area, a rest room and the challenge of climbing the steep mile-long trail to the summit.

At this summit, too, a panoramic view unfolds. Hang-gliders hang out here, too. But only long enough to get the courage to hurl themselves off the mountain to land in the parking area below.

Both parks are open weekends starting Memorial Day, and daily from early June through October. A fee is charged.

A sweeping birch tree graces the idyllic picnic grounds at Winslow State Park.

Rollins and Winslow State Parks

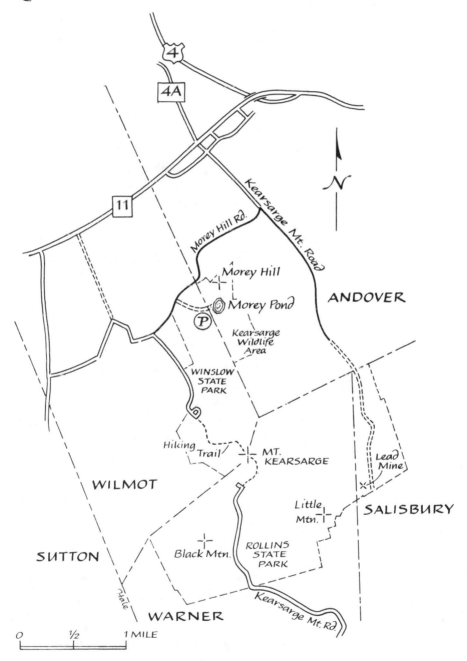

4

4A

11

Kearsarge Mt. Road

Morey Hill Rd.

Morey Hill

Morey Pond

P

Kearsarge
Wildlife
Area

ANDOVER

WINSLOW
STATE
PARK

N

Hiking Trail

MT.
KEARSARGE

Lead
Mine

WILMOT

Little
Mtn.

SALISBURY

SUTTON

Black Mtn.

ROLLINS
STATE
PARK

Hale

WARNER

Kearsarge Mt. Rd.

0   ½   1 MILE

Ride Information

> **Ride Level:** Beginner.
> **Trail Distances:** 11-mile out-and-back ride. Other options.
> **Trail Descriptions:** Some packed gravel town roads with little car traffic. Trails are double-track, pine-needle covered trails. Some paved roads. Fairly level, flat.
> **Highlights:** Magnificent views. Picnic area. Hiking trails. Super family spot. Great birch stands. Wildlife. Possible moose sighting at Morey Pond if you're an early riser.
> **Start:** Park your car at the Winslow State Park area. It's three and a half miles south of Wilmot Flat, off Route 11. You'll see a sign indicating Winslow State Park. Turn right into the parking area by Morey Pond.
> **Note:** A fee is charged at both Winslow and Rollins State Parks. Please stay on trails designated on the map. The surrounding area is private property.

Ride Options

1. Morey Hill-Kearsarge Mountain Road Ride. This is an 11-mile out-and-back ride. From the parking area by Morey Pond, take a left on Morey Hill a half mile past the park entrance. (Or go as far as you'd like.) For this ride to be around 11 miles, you will need to turn around and head back at this point. Continue past the Kearsarge entrance to Kearsarge Mountain Road on the right. Take a right. You can travel on this wonderful double-track road with picturesque birches and sun-dappled pathways for miles. Often moose are sighted in the bogs. Also be aware that you may encounter some wet areas due to beavers damming-up a stream.

You'll pass a New Hampshire Fish and Game cabin on this road. There are a few gradual climbs. When you reach the lead mine on your right, stop and turn around. Beyond it you're on private property and are not welcome. Please respect the rights of private property owners.

2. Cilleyville Road. Instead of going right at the Cilleyville Road/ Kearsarge Mountain Road intersection, go left. Go as far as you'd like.

CHAPTER 16

SUGAR RIVER TRAIL

If you want to experience northern New England life at its best, visit the Dartmouth-Lake Sunapee Region of New Hampshire. Here, on the eastern side of the Connecticut River which forms the border between New Hampshire and Vermont, you'll find things are still much the way they used to be—a beautiful, unspoiled countryside of rolling farmland, small villages, town greens with gazebos and town squares, and traditional values that still hold strong.

The area has much to offer. Recreation from hiking and biking to swimming and skiing. Super theater and art museums. Famous sculptor Augustus Saint-Gaudens made his home in Cornish. His studio and gardens are a place for a leisure visit. The grounds are replete with replicas of many of his works. The house and studio sit on a sweep of lawn with views of Mt. Ascutney.

August ushers in the annual Craftsmen's Fair at Mt. Sunapee State Park. Boasting its claim to fame, the oldest crafts fair in the nation, the event draws crowds from all over New England and the East Coast. Other points of interest include Plummer Ledge Natural Area in Wentworth, Sculpted Rock Natural Area in Groton, The Fells Historic Site at the John Hay National Wildlife Refuge in Newbury, the Franklin Pierce Homestead Historic Site in Hillsboro, and Ruggles Mine in Grafton.

This area of the state offers an abundance of covered bridges—16, in fact. One is the longest wooden bridge in the U.S. and the longest

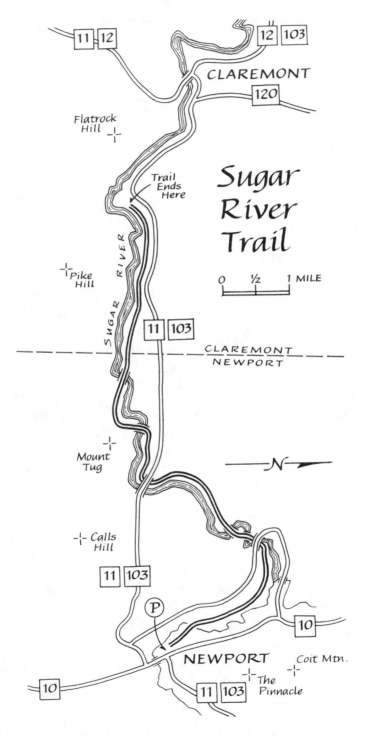

11 12   12 103

CLAREMONT

120

Flatrock
Hill

Trail
Ends
Here

Sugar
River
Trail

SUGAR RIVER

Pike
Hill

0   ½   1 MILE

11 103

CLAREMONT
NEWPORT

Mount
Tug

N

Calls
Hill

11 103

P

10

NEWPORT   Coit Mtn.

The
Pinnacle

10   11 103

two-span covered bridge in the world. It's the Cornish-Windsor Bridge. If you feel like seeing them all, get hold of a free copy of *The Official New Hampshire Guidebook* by calling the New Hampshire Office of Travel and Tourism Department at 603 271-2666, or write them at P.O. Box 1856, Concord, NH 03302-1856. A full list of covered bridges is included in the guide.

Two bridges not mentioned in the guide you will get to explore on your Sugar River Trail bike ride. The reason they're not mentioned in the guidebook is because they are not accessible by car. They're railroad covered bridges. Of the only five remaining historical covered railroad bridges left in the U.S., you will travel through two of them on this ride. The trail follows the Sugar River along a former railroad bed between Newport and Claremont. This breathtaking, 20-mile (out-and-back) Sugar River Trail ride is perfect for a family. The terrain is nearly flat. The views of the river are grand. You can still see remains of railroad history. Pay attention and you'll see the historic granite mile markers that line the path, along with an occasional railroad spike.

Fred McLaughlin

Of only five historic covered railroad bridges left in the entire country, you'll pass through two on this ride.

Just off the trail are numerous places for a picnic. The area is stunning during foliage season.

Ride Information

Ride Level:	Novice and intermediate.
Trail Distances:	20 miles out-and-back. Can be shorter by turning around sooner.
Trail Descriptions:	Former railroad bed. Ties have been removed. A smooth, flat ride. Mostly well-packed dirt. Some loose sand.
Highlights:	Nice views of the river. Picnic areas along the trail. Super family spot.
Start:	From the center of Newport go north on Route 10 for .2-mile, turn left on Belknap Avenue. You'll see an OHV sign. Parking area is .1-mile on the right between Ransom's Furniture Store and the Newport Recreation Department. Trail starts at the north end of the parking lot by a propane tank.
Note:	No fee to ride this trail. The trail is multiple use, so you may encounter motorcycles and ATVs.

Ride Options

1. Sugar River Trail (out-and-back). This is a 20-mile round-trip ride. The first part of the trail you go through the backyards of some homes. Less than half a mile in you'll cross an old iron railroad bridge. As you ride along you will see mile markers and other artifacts from a bygone era.

At the 2.7, 2.9 and 3.2 mile mark, you'll cross iron bridges. All of the bridges have solid decking so it is easy riding. Soon you cross under Route 11 and Route 103. The first covered bridge is at 6.1 miles. You will notice that the bridge is much taller than other covered bridges you have seen. This is, of course, to allow the large train engine passage, and also to leave enough room for the smoke from the steam engines to dissipate without causing a fire from sparks.

The second railroad covered bridge is at mile 7.3. The trail ends alongside Route 11 and Route 103 at 10 miles. Turn around and retrace your ride back to the parking lot.

SOUTHERN REGION

CHAPTER 17

MAST YARD STATE FOREST

W ho says bigger is better? Mast Yard State Forest is a little-known 636-acre forest located in Concord and Hopkinton. There's no ranger station. No beach. No concession stand. No crowds either. This small forest is a super location for a family ride. You're on trails with no traffic. You just pedal easily along on a flat surface alongside the Claremont-Concord Railroad tracks. Deer are abundant in this forest. Keep your eyes peeled. You may see some.

Mast Yard State Forest was used as a mast yard during colonial times—up until the Revolution—for trees for ship masts for the King of England. The trees were dragged by oxen to the yard, the limbs were removed and then they were floated down the river to Massachusetts where they were transported by ship to England.

The trail network at Mast Yard State Forest is about 10 miles of too-easy biking. You have a number of options. A quick look at the map shows you can do out-and-backs. You can do a number of different loops. You can ride on the gravel roads also. Another choice is to ride along the power line. You're off state property when you follow the power line, but riding under them is permitted.

If you'd like to combine this with other activities in the area, Concord proper is just down the road a piece and offers many options. Check out Chapter 9 for some suggestions.

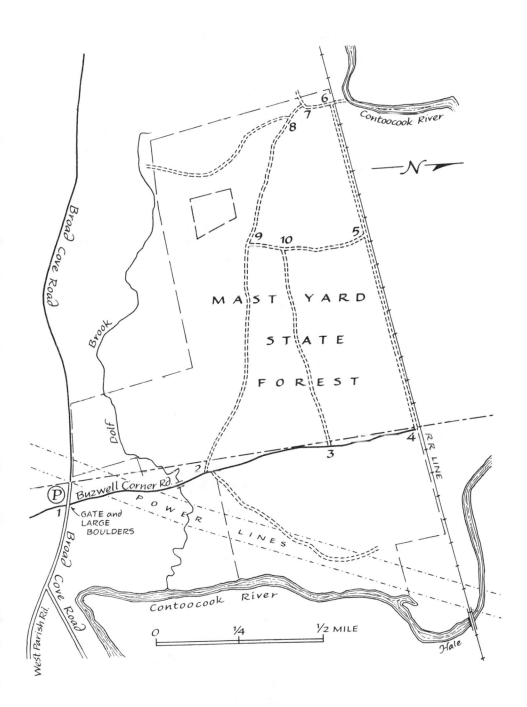

Contoocook River

N

Broad Cove Road

Brook

Dolf

MAST YARD

STATE

FOREST

R.R. LINE

6
7
8
5
9 10
4
3
2
P Buzwell Corner Rd.
1
GATE and
LARGE
BOULDERS

POWER   LINES

Broad Cove Road

West Parish Rd.

Contoocook   River

Hale

0   ¼   ½ MILE

Mast Yard State Forest

Ride Information

Ride Level:	Novice and intermediate.
Trail Distances:	As much as 10 miles if you ride all the trails.
Trail Descriptions:	Gravel or packed dirt. One stretch is alongside railroad tracks.
Highlights:	Quiet. Possible deer sightings. Good for family ride or novice who wants open space. Close to Concord and other Capital Region attractions.
Start:	In Hopkinton, take Penacook Road west off Route 103. At T, go right on Briar Hill Road for half a mile. Turn left on Broad Cove Road (gravel) for 1.5 miles to an intersection. There's a gate here with large boulders. Park here.
Note:	No fee to ride in Mast Yard State Forest.

Ride Options

For easier communication, some intersections are numbered on the map.

1. Big Loop. This 4-mile loop takes you along the Claremont-Concord Railroad tracks. From the parking lot, you go to intersection 2, 4, 6, 7, 2 and back to 1.

2. Little Loop. For the faint of heart or for a quick ride to check out a demo bike, do this abbreviated loop. Start at parking area, go to intersection 3, 10, 9, 2 and back to the parking area.

3. Spur Roads. Several spur roads can be explored. At intersection 2 you can take a right and ride for a mile before the trail ends. At intersection 8 a spur road leads you nearly to Dolf Brook before it terminates.

4. Town Roads. If you want to add to your mileage and enjoyment, consider some of the town roads. Broad Cove Road is a maintained gravel road. Numerous paved roads also crisscross this area.

5. Power Line Trails. Near the parking area you can enter the trails that follow beneath the power line. The trail can go on for miles. Riding under them is not restricted here.

CHAPTER 18

VINCENT STATE FOREST

There's only one Henniker in the world, and if you choose this ride, you get to go there! Henniker is home of picturesque New England College. This sprawling campus is sprinkled among the rolling hills of the small New England village—complete with a photo-opportunity covered bridge near the center of town.

Vincent State Forest is a beautiful area tucked in the folds of Pat's Peak off Route 114—in Henniker. This small forest with 626 acres is really a find—provided you can find it. It's a bit tricky to get there as the roads are not well marked and they blend together. But asking the locals for directions is OK.

You roll along for miles on well-packed town gravel roads or pine-needle covered trails flanked on both sides by stone walls. The forest offers numerous options. If you're a novice and interested in only smooth roads, stay off the trails and on the gravel roads. But for the more adventurous, take on North Road and Sawdust Pile Trail, where you'll maneuver around embedded and loose rocks, and wet conditions in the spring. The trails are hilly at times. Beginners, if you *still* want to do this, just walk your bikes around these areas and push your bikes up the hills.

The trail network on the map is about five miles of riding. But add some runs on the numerous gravel roads (that have little traffic) adjacent to the forest, and you will increase your mileage substantially. I'd suggest picking up a detailed local map. The area is confusing and you could find yourself traveling in circles.

Vincent State Forest

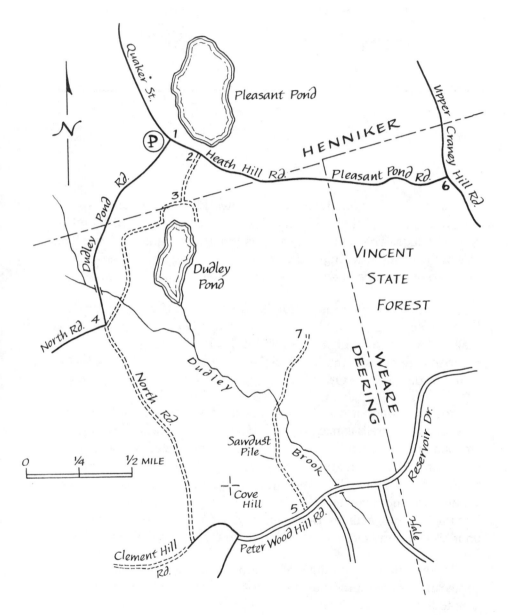

If you'd like to combine this with other activities in the area, Concord is not too far away and offers many options. Check out Chapter 9 for some suggestions.

Ride Information

Ride Level:	Novice and intermediate.
Trail Distances:	5 miles of mapped trails, but you have to return on some as they're not loops, so your mileage will increase. Additionally, many gravel roads offer unlimited opportunity for more mileage.
Trail Discriptions:	Gravel or packed dirt. Some embedded rocks. Some loose rocks. Some erosion-created ruts. Wet areas particularly in the spring.
Highlights:	Quiet, pretty area. Scenic, too. Close to Concord.
Start:	Just before you enter Henniker on Route 114N, turn left on Gulf Road. Then right on Flanders. At fork, stay right, then go left on Quaker Street. Quaker Street becomes gravel. Park at fork at Dudley Pond Road and Quaker Street/Heath Hill Road. This is tricky to find. The roads aren't well-marked and they blend into the next road and change names. Welcome to New England!
Note:	No fee to ride in Vincent State Forest.

Ride Options

For easier communication, some intersections are numbered on the map.

1. Dudley Pond Loop. This is a warm-up loop of 2 miles. The ride begins on a gravel road with very little car traffic. From intersection 1, you go to intersection 4, 3, 2 and back to 1. You'll have some downhill areas from 3-2-1. For more of a challenge, go clockwise on this loop.

2. Pleasant Pond Road. This is a 2.2-mile out-and-back trip. The trail is flanked by aging stone walls on both sides. At the end of this trail are a couple of houses. It seems like private property, but it is public land as long as you remain on the trail. To get there, go from intersection 1 to 6 and back.

4. Almost-a-Loop Trail. This ride is "almost a loop." Start at intersection 1, go to 4, 5, 7 and back. The pine-needled trails are wonderful to ride on. It's the perfect way to commune with nature—cruising along quiet trails with the twitter of songbirds in the background and an occasional chipmunk startling you back to reality.

Dudley Pond Road is a gravel road with some car traffic. It blends into North Road which is not maintained and becomes more challenging. It has embedded and loose rocks and is wet in the spring.

At intersection 5, you can take Sawdust Pile Trail left. It seems foreboding because a gate is located here. It bears a sign that says "Private Road No Trespassing." Ignore it. The state forester for the region says the road is on state property and is accessible to the public.

5. Town Gravel Roads. All along here are lots of town gravel roads. They see little traffic and present a large network of additional trails to ride. Enjoy and try not to get lost!

6. Nearby. Just down the road—on Chase Road near the Butter Road intersection is Totten Trails State Forest. It is fabulous for family outings. See the next chapter for details.

The trail isn't terribly long, but combine it with these Vincent State Forest trails or bring the family along and make a day of it. Totten Trails State Forest has mowed grassy trails popular with hikers and is a super place for a picnic lunch.

CHAPTER 19

TOTTEN TRAILS STATE FOREST

This isn't the smallest forest in the state, but it is one of them. Totten Trails State Forest proudly boasts 109 acres of attractive grass knolls that hikers flock to and picnickers hope no one finds out about. It's a short trail for mountain bike riding located in Henniker very near Vincent State Forest. The best way to take advantage of this forest is to combine it with Vincent. Cruise the mountain bike trails at Vincent State Forest and then to Totten Trails State Forest for a short ride and/or picnic. (See Chapter 18 for the scoop on Vincent State Forest.)

The in-and-out trail at Vincent is 1.2 miles. You can add some runs on the numerous gravel roads here and increase your mileage substantially. The roads have little car traffic. I'd suggest picking up a detailed local map. The area is confusing and you could find yourself traveling in circles.

If you want to ride your bike over from Vincent Forest, take Quaker Street to Huntington Road, to Butter Road to Chase Road. See map.

You might even want to make a weekend of it. Maybe stay at a bed and breakfast, like the Colby Hill Inn (603 428-3281) in Henniker, a lovely Federal home that leans a bit here and there, which only adds to its charm. Or try The Meeting House (603 428-3228), where you can also indulge in some whitewater activities on the Contoocook River or enjoy summer theater in nearby towns.

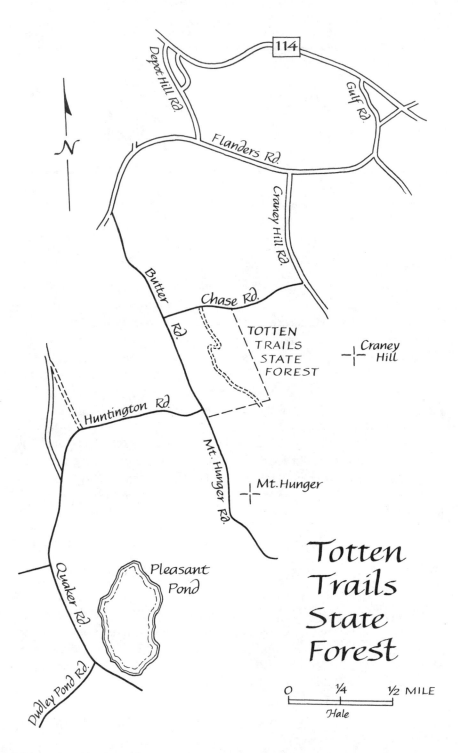

114

Depot Hill Rd.

Gulf Rd.

N

Flanders Rd.

Craney Hill Rd.

Butter Rd.

Chase Rd.

TOTTEN
TRAILS
STATE
FOREST

Craney
Hill

Huntington Rd.

Mt. Hunger Rd.

Mt. Hunger

Quaker Rd.

Pleasant
Pond

Totten
Trails
State
Forest

Dudley Pond Rd.

0   ¼   ½ MILE

Hale

If you'd like to combine this with other activities in the area, Concord is not too far away and offers many options. Check out Chapter 9 for some suggestions.

Ride Information:

Ride Level:	Novice.
Trail Distances:	1.2 miles in-and-out. Combine with nearby Vincent State Forest for additional mileage or ride the maze of gravel roads in the area.
Trail Discriptions:	Grassy, mowed trail. Easy traveling.
Highlights:	Great for family event. This area is popular for picnics. Close to Concord.
Start:	Just before you enter Henniker on Route 114N, turn left on Gulf Road. Then right on Flanders. At fork, left on Butter Road. Next intersection is Chase Road. Left on Chase. A short way from intersection on right is the trail.
Note:	No fee to ride in Totten Trails State Forest.

Ride Options

1. Out-and-Back Trail. This is a 1.2-mile ride in-and-out. Super for kids or those getting to know their bike. It's also great for picnicking or just hiking about. It's a lovely setting with mowed grass and pastoral clearings. Great photo-opportunities in the fall when New England parades around in her best foliage attire.

2. Vincent State Forest: Nearby. Combine your time at Totten Trail State Forest with nearby Vincent. See information in previous chapter for directions on how to get there.

3. Town Gravel Roads. All along here are lots of town gravel roads. They see little traffic and present a large network of additional trails to ride. Enjoy and try not to get lost!

CHAPTER 20

PILLSBURY STATE PARK

Black diamond! Well, it's not as threatening as a terrifying downhill ski slope, but this area is for experts only. Old logging trails, rugged terrain, and wet areas challenge even the serious mountain biker.

Pillsbury State Park is due west of Concord in Washington, NH. Washington, the first town to incorporate in 1776 under the leadership of George Washington, is a classic New England village. Pillsbury State Park is a relatively undisturbed wilderness of woods, ponds, wetlands and hills. Farmers who settled here called the area Cherry Valley because of the abundance of cherry trees. The numerous ponds and their water power to run sawmills, attracted lumbering to the valley in the 1780s. Despite the bounteous lumber supply, the mills still suffered hard times. Fire was an ever-present danger. The economic instability of a young nation encouraged clear cutting and scarcity of lumber during boom times, followed by neglect when the economy turned sour.

One of the last mill owners, Albert E. Pillsbury, was one of the founders of the Society for the Protection of New Hampshire Forests, an organization dedicated to preserving wetlands and protecting the state's natural scenery. He purchased 2,400 acres of cut-over land in Cherry Valley in 1905. But 10 years later popular concern about clear cutting and stream pollution from sawdust and mill refuse brought his mills to a screeching halt. Pillsbury's diversity of interests took a turn away from his forest property and in 1920 he deeded the land to the public as a "public forest reservation."

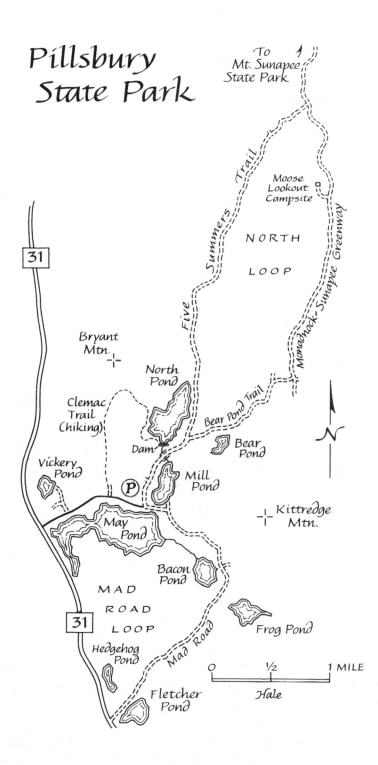

Pillsbury State Park

To Mt. Sunapee State Park

Moose Lookout Campsite

NORTH LOOP

Five Summers Trail

Monadnock-Sunapee Greenway

31

Bryant Mtn.

North Pond

Clemac Trail (hiking)

Bear Pond Trail

Dam

Bear Pond

Vickery Pond

P

Mill Pond

May Pond

Kittredge Mtn.

Bacon Pond

MAD ROAD LOOP

31

Mad Road

Frog Pond

Hedgehog Pond

Fletcher Pond

N

0   ½   1 MILE

Hale

Over the years various state agencies managed the land. Then in 1935 the Civilian Conservation Commission restored and rebuilt several dams. Today Pillsbury State Park is a wilderness park of more than 5,000 acres where wild ducks frequent the ponds where sawdust once clogged the waters. Hiking and mountain biking are popular, along with picnicking, fishing, camping and bird watching.

And the wildlife is prolific! Pillsbury provides habitat for moose, bear, deer, fisher and otter. The marshes and bogs in the park attract Great Blue Heron, harriers and osprey. The forests sing with songbirds—redstarts, Philadelphia vireos, pine warblers and ovenbirds. And a New Hampshire favorite inhabits the ponds, the common loon.

The park is a vital link in the Monadnock Sunapee Greenway, a 51-mile trail between these two parks.

Ride Information

Ride Level:	Expert.
Trail Distances:	Loop rides of 6.5 or 8 miles. Or try some out-and-back choices.
Trail Descriptions:	Challenging. Bumpy riding, some rocks, ruts and long ascents. But some smooth riding, scenic areas too. Some areas require carrying your bike.
Highlights:	Picnic areas, camping, fishing, birding.
Start:	Heading north, take exit 5 off I-89. Follow Route 9 west through Hillsborough to Route 31. Turn right (north) on Route 31. Park entrance is 4 miles north of Washington center. Park by Mad Road Trail and "The Tree." (Toilet facilities at visitor center.)
Note:	Fee is charged for campsite use. You share trails with hikers.

Ride Options

1. Mad Road Loop. 6.5-mile loop. From the parking area by Mill Pond, cross the footbridge to Mad Road. A pleasant, rolling trail under paper birch trees and spreading beech trees, the grass grows up in the center of the road as you meander past Bacon Pond. You'll encounter a half-mile climb, then a descent on a rutty slope. The road levels off and you come to Route 31. Route 31 is paved and downhill! You cruise easily along back to the entrance and back to the parking area.

2. North Loop. 8-mile loop. This really is for the experienced mountain biker. You have to have the stamina and skill to deal with the terrain. But if you do, you're going to love this! Take Five Summers Trail, so-dubbed because it took that long to construct it during the 1950s. (That's a hint, guys. Are you ready for this?) The trail climbs on old logging trails, passes North Pond spur and Clemac Trail (They're ok for hiking, but not rideable by bike), and Ts at Monadnock Sunapee Greenway. Go right on this trail. (Going left will take you to Mt. Sunapee State Park.) White tree blazes mark the course. You will need to carry your bike when the slopes are too steep.

Farther along on the Greenway, the trail follows a ridge which divides the Connecticut and Merrimack river valleys. Many sections are surprisingly smooth as you glide along through the hardwood forest, sunlight filtering through the branches overhead. You intersect with Bear Pond Trail (blazed in blue), and it gets trickier. Go right on Bear Pond Trail. Erosion has caused steep areas and you must carefully navigate through the washouts. Then you encounter wet spots. Finally you reach your point of origin back at the parking lot.

3. Out-and-Back Trails. If, back at the intersection of the Greenway trail and Bear Pond Trail in the ride above, you continue straight (south) on the Greenway, you can go all the way to Washington. New Hampshire, that is. Near Kittredge Mountain, hiking is required. Rock formations and trees present an obstacle course. Then uphill climbs challenge your skills. But finally stone walls along the path, picturesque sugar maples, and ponds teeming with occasionally seen wildlife provide a ride all worth the effort.

CHAPTER 21

NORTHWOOD MEADOWS STATE PARK

History in the making—that's Northwood Meadows State Park. This park is purported to be the first of its kind in the country. Why? It's universally accessible. Acquired by the state in 1991, this 600-acre park in Northwood, east of Concord, is still in-process. The plan is to have it wheelchair accessible. Hundreds of Telephone Pioneers of America volunteers have already donated time and energy to clear trails, build fishing piers and create gradual inclines to canoe and rowboat launching areas. Plans are to add picnic tables and an environmental education center.

The park offers something for everyone. It's perfect for the beginner mountain biker or a family with little mountain bikers. You can experience nature, take a walk under the tall pines, have a picnic lunch and get some exercise all within the confines of this little-known wilderness nature area. The path around Meadow Lake is only a mile and half. It's flat, too. If you want more challenge, other options can put mileage, mud and mystery into your ride. Mileage because you can put 10 miles on your bike with a large loop. Mud because you'll ride through some. And mystery because you're not sure where you'll come out if you make a wrong turn. But that's part of the adventure of mountain biking.

Northwood
Meadows
State
Park

202 9
4

Kelsey Mill Rd.

Blake's Hill Road

Coffeetown Rd.

HARVEY
LAKE

Harmony Rd.

MEADOW LAKE

P

P

Dashingdown Rd.

DEMON
POND

Mountain Road

202
9
4

43

202 9

4

0   ½   1 MILE

Hale

Ride Information

Ride Level:	Novice. Some intermediate and expert challenges.
Trail Distances:	Short ride around lake is 1.5 miles. Larger loop 3.5 miles. Town roads and trails can add more mileage.
Trail Descriptions:	Pine-needle covered trails. Some dirt trails, wet, rocky areas. Flat, family-appropriate. Buggy—bring spray.
Highlights:	Picnic areas, fishing, boating, hiking.
Start:	Park entrance is on Route 4 in Northwood, a mile east of Coe-Brown Academy. A large sign indicates entrance. Additional parking inside the park.
Note:	No fee is charged. Carry-in, carry-out trash policy. Gate locked at dusk. Toilets.

Ride Options

1. Meadow Lake Loop. 1.5-mile loop. Novice level. Terrific for families. (If you park your car at the Route 4 entrance, you'll add a mile to this ride.) This ride hugs the lake shore. It's rolling with a few rocks.

2. Western Extension Loop. 3.5-mile loop. Several fishing piers are located along this loop which also circles the lake—it's just a larger loop than option 1. The piers are great for picnics. The Western Extension trail is smooth and relatively flat. You glide quietly along on pine-needle covered trails under towering pine tress. A few spur (side) roads are off the main road, but they are very short.

The eastern side of this loop has some short, steep hills.

3. Out-and-About Trails. More challenging is Mountain Road. It has a long, gradual hill and then a steep hill, and then levels off. If you take it to the left, rolling terrain will take you over rocks and puddles. After 3 miles you hit a dirt road, and eventually pavement. You intersect with Route 43—a paved road. You're about 4 miles away from your car. To get back to the park entrance and your car, go left to Route 4. Turn left again, on Route 4. Entrance will be on your left.

Several roads off Mountain Road can also be explored.

4. More Out-and-About Trails. A number of country backroads are also possibilities. A snowmobile trail between Demon Pond and Mountain Road on Dashingdown Road offers additional riding.

On the other side of the map, Mountain Road leads over to town roads. Harmony Road and Blake's Hill Road can extend your travels. You can go out-and-back or get on Route 4 and do a loop back to the park entrance.

CHAPTER 22

HONEY BROOK STATE FOREST

Unspoiled countryside. Quiet. Picturesque, small villages. That's what it's like in the Connecticut River Valley of New Hampshire. This state forest just north of Keene is tucked in the farmlands and meadows just east of the Connecticut River. The forest is a nature lover's—and photographer's—delight. A beaver pond offers an opportunity to watch nature at work. Moose are often seen here early mornings. Red and white pine form the perfect natural setting for a picnic. Ancient stone walls provide a study in texture and light for the photographer. Light dappling through the pines throws intricate contrasting patterns on the pine-needled ground. And the scent—heavenly.

Honey Brook Forest covers 975 acres in the towns of Acworth, Marlow and Lempster. If you do the loop, the ride is partially on paved roads and partially on trails. Going out and back is also an option. The map for this ride also includes Dodge Brook State Forest. (See Chapter 23 for more details.) Because they both offer limited riding trails, they were placed on the same map to encourage you to ride down the road a piece and do both areas. The riding level for the two rides is advanced beginner or intermediate. A 200-foot stretch of trail is washed out but navigable on the edge. There are some rocks and ascents.

Ride Information

           Ride Level: Advanced beginner and intermediate.
Trail Distances: Loop ride: 6 miles. Town roads and trails can add
                       more mileage.

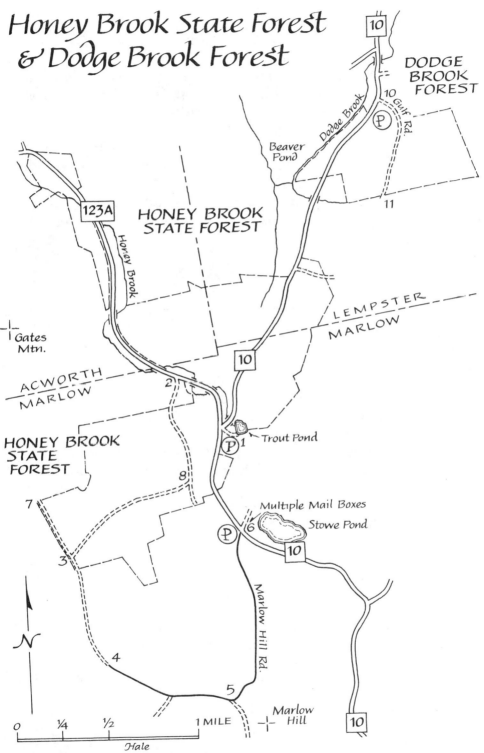

Honey Brook State Forest & Dodge Brook Forest

10

DODGE BROOK FOREST

10 Gulf Rd.

Dodge Brook

Beaver Pond

123A

HONEY BROOK STATE FOREST

Honey Brook

11

LEMPSTER
MARLOW

Gates Mtn.

ACWORTH
MARLOW

10

2

Trout Pond

P 1

HONEY BROOK STATE FOREST

8

7

Multiple Mail Boxes

Stowe Pond

P 6

10

3

Marlow Hill Rd.

N

4

5

Marlow Hill

0   ¼   ½   1 MILE

Hale

10

115

Trail Descriptions: Pine-needle covered trails. Some single-track wet, rocky areas. Trail washed out in some areas.

Highlights: Quiet, nature area.

Start: Park in one of three areas. **One:** park at intersection of Route 123A and 10 in Marlow. Park on right off road. **Two:** From 123A/10 intersection, go north .3 mile on 123A . Park on left by trail. **Three:** .9 mile before 123A/10 intersection on Route 10. Multiple mail boxes at this corner. No formal entrance to forest.

Note: No fee is charged. State forest property is marked with blue blazes on trees. Respect private property.

Ride Options

For easier communication, some intersections are numbered on the map.

1. Marlow Hill Road Loop. 6-mile loop. Advanced beginner to intermediate. You won't want to bring small children on this loop. There are washed-out and wet areas to contend with. But it's a scenic ride and worth all your effort. Start from the parking area on Route 10 by the multiple mailboxes (intersection 6), take Marlow Hill Road, a gravel town road with little traffic. It bends around to your right as you go to intersection 5 and 4. At area 4 you'll see a couple of houses on the hill to your left. Continue straight on what looks like a driveway, soon you'll see the trail ahead of you. A rock wall is on your right. The gravel road ends here and a single track trail that is wet in spots begins. At intersection 3, turn right. (If you want, you can explore the spur road down to area 7 and back.) At intersection 8 go left along the rock wall to intersection 2. Turn right on Route 123A back to intersection 6.

2. Trout Pond Out-and-Back. From parking area at Route 123A/10, follow the trail into the woods a short way to the trout pond.

3. Dodge Brook Forest. See the next chapter for details. Take Route 10 north 2 miles to Dodge Brook Forest. (Included on this map.)

CHAPTER 23

DODGE BROOK STATE FOREST

A treat to the olfactory senses. That's what Dodge Brook State Forest has in store for you. The scent of pine is heavenly.

Dodge Brook is another small forest in New Hampshire that is easily missed. You could drive right past it and never know it's a forest. But it is, and the state welcomes the visiting public to enjoy it. Just down the road from Honey Brook State Forest, Dodge Brook has a short double-track in-and-out trail lined with stone walls on both sides, a few moderate climbs and the potential to see moose. The trail is a bit more than a mile round trip.

Ride Information

Ride Level: Beginner and intermediate.

Trail Distances: Loop ride: 1.2 miles out-and-back.

Trail Descriptions: Double-track trail. Some climbing.

Highlights: Quiet, nature area.

Start: (See last chapter directions.) From 123A/10 intersection, go north 2.2 miles on Route 10. Park on right by gravel pit and birch stand. Forest property is marked with blue blazes on trees. Don't go beyond the .6 miles in because it's then private property.

Note: No fee is charged. Best to combine this with Honey Brook State Forest, Chapter 22. Map is also in Chapter 22.

117

Ride Options

Because this is a short trail, only 1.2 miles in-and-out, you probably should combine it with Honey Brook State Forest, which is 2 miles south on Route 10. The map for Dodge Brook is with Honey Brook, Chapter 22.

1. Dodge Brook out-and-back trail. 1.2 miles. This is a super trail for mountain biking. A gradual ascent gives you a workout. There are some wet areas. Moose are often sighted here—if you're an early riser.

Go from intersection 10 to 11 and back.

2. Honey Brook Forest. See previous chapter for details. Honey Brook is 2 miles south and offers more biking trails.

CHAPTER 24

FOX STATE FOREST

W hile it may look like just another forest, Fox State Forest holds status in the forestry world. Established in the 1930s by Caroline Fox, who gave the state the land and a trust fund to maintain it, the forest was primarily a research forest for the state. The forest hosted scientists from around the world and remained active as a research facility through the 1970s. The forest is home to Mud Pond Bog, a glacial kettlehole (formed during the Ice Age when a glacier deposited a large ice mass) and rare tupelo trees in Black-Gum Swamp (found more prominently in the south). Natural areas are scattered throughout the forest.

Hillsboro, where Fox State Forest is located, straddles the Contoocook River and is a narrow valley town. Recreational trails have been built in the forest over the years. But until recently the forest was known only to the locals, foresters and a few skiers and recreationists.

Spectacular views of Mt. Monadnock, Mt. Riley, Crotched Mountain, Hedgehog Hill and Clark Summit (Wolf Hill), are ready for your picture album looking south from Munroe Tower.

Mountain bike riders will find there are no easy rides in Fox Forest. Difficult sections with roots, rocks, ledges and uphill climbs are the norm. The woods roads (Hurricane, Proctor, Harvey roads) are in great shape and super for the less technical rider.

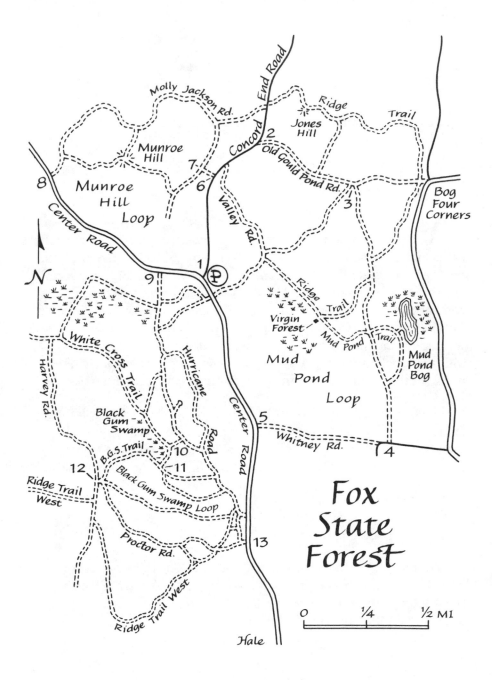

Molly Jackson Rd.

Concord End Road

Ridge Trail

Jones Hill

Munroe Hill

Old Gould Pond Rd.

Munroe Hill Loop

Valley Rd.

Center Road

Bog Four Corners

N

Ridge Trail

Virgin Forest

Mud Pond Trail

Mud Pond Bog

Mud Pond Loop

White Cross Trail

Harvey Rd.

Hurricane Road

Center Road

Black Gum Swamp

B.G.S. Trail

Whitney Rd.

Ridge Trail West

Black Gum Swamp Loop

Proctor Rd.

Ridge Trail West

Hale

Fox State Forest

0   ¼   ½ MI

120

Ride Information

Ride Level:	Intermediate and advanced.
Trail Distances:	2.5-, 4- and 6-mile loop rides. The forest offers 25+ miles of trails.
Trail Descriptions:	Gravel roads, single-track, double-track and some paved roads. Rocks, erosion and ledges.
Highlights:	Super views of mountains. Walking and hiking trails. Good bird watching. Rare trees and eco-systems. Glacial kettlehole (Mud Pond Bog.) Picnicking. Educational programs and forestry museum.
Start:	From the center of Hillsboro, drive 2 miles north on Center Road. The forest entrance is on the right.
Note:	No fee is charged. State forest trails are well-marked. The forest is a popular destination for a variety of activities, so be aware of other people on the trails. Signs indicating "No Wheeled Vehicles" refer to motorized vehicles.

Ride Options

For easier communication, some intersections are numbered on the map.

1. Munroe Hill Loop. Advanced rider. This 2.5-mile loop begins at the parking lot (intersection 1), and then north to intersection 6, 7 (where you go right and loop around) to intersection 8. Back to the parking lot at intersection 1.

An elaboration of the above loop: As you leave the parking lot on Concord End Road, you descend for a quarter of a mile, then take a steep left climb to Spring Road. A right on Spring Road climbs past a spring house on the left. This spring and one other fed several farms in the last century. Spring Road diminishes to a single track trail and circles around Munroe Hill. At one point the trail drops down over a steep, short ledge. You will cross an old logging operation and come to a trail junction. If you go straight, it takes you to Munroe Tower overlook with great views to the south of half a dozen mountain peaks.

As you continue on Ridge Trail to intersection 8, you will descend on an increasingly steep, but smooth, logging road. Go left at Center Road (intersection 8) back to the parking area.

2. Black Gum Swamp Loop. 4 miles. From parking lot take Center Road to intersection 9. Then left on 9 to 10, 11, 12, 13 and back to 1.

An elaboration of the above loop: Hurricane Road is so-called because is was used to salvage timber after the Hurricane of '38. Take Hurricane Road to the height of the land and then take the trail to the right. You will see a sign that says "Overlook." This affords views of Bear Hill, Craney Hill and a nice panorama of Rosewald Farm below. Continue on the trail as noted above to intersection 12, and go right on Proctor Road. At 13, take a left back to the parking area.

3. Mud Pond Loop. 6-mile loop. From parking area, go to intersection 6, 2, 3, 4, 5 and back to 1.

Concord End Road takes you to the intersection with Old Gould Pond Road where you'll go right on Mud Pond Road. Washouts are common fare along this road until it levels near Mud Pond. The pond is a state natural area. It's the glacial kettlehole mentioned earlier in the text. At Whitney Road, go right. It's a double-track trail flanked with stone walls back to Center Road, Right on Center takes you back to the parking area.

3. Other Trail Options. The trails on the map are all options. Fox State Forest is a favorite with mountain bikers who all have trails they prefer. Come out, explore and see what ones you want to ride again and again.

CHAPTER 25

CLOUGH STATE PARK

F loods were an all too common spring occurrence along the Piscataquog River in the Merrimack River Basin until the Army Corps of Engineers built the Hopkinton and Everett dams. Completed in 1962 at a cost of $21.4 million, the dams control flood waters in Concord, Manchester, and Nashua, New Hampshire, and Lowell, Lawrence and Haverhill, Massachusetts. The river was stabilized by building Everett Dam and created 150-acre Everett Lake, now the site of Clough State Park.

Clough State Park in Weare is embedded within the Hopkinton-Everett Reservoir. Riding in the park is limited to the paved road. However, a system of dirt roads and trails run throughout Hopkinton-Everett Reservoir. We're keeping a narrow focus on Clough in this Chapter, but open it up for "the expanded version" in Chapter 26, where we cover the Hopkinton-Everett Reservoir at-large. The distinction is also in the riding trails. Clough State is geared more to the leisure rider, while Chapter 26's Hopkinton-Everett rides fit a far more experienced mountain biker. In fact, a friend calls some of its trails, "Double Black Diamonds." (Those of you who aren't skiers, one black diamond on a trail denotes expert level.)

The trail system is a cooperative effort of the U.S. Army Corps of Engineers, NH Department of Resources and Economic Development Trails Bureau, and Merrimack Valley Trail Riders. Trails are used by motorized bikes and mountain bikes.

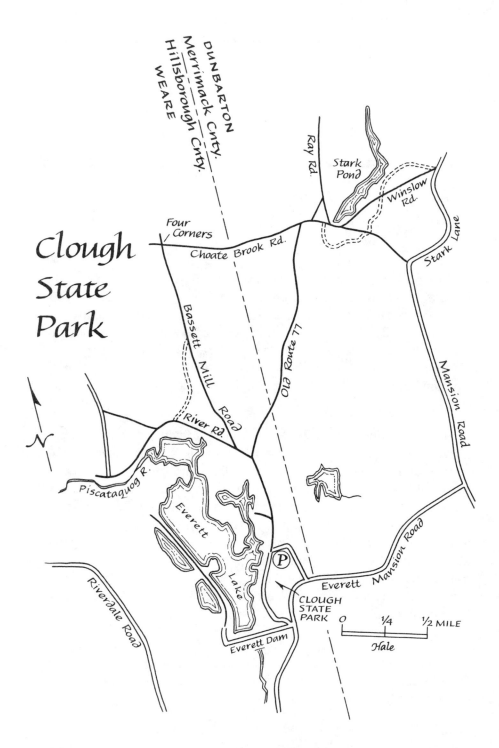

Clough
State
Park

This is a multi-purpose park. A sandy beach invites swimming. Rental boats encourage a relaxing fishing expedition. A large picnic grove and playground provide distraction for the kids. And don't miss the Everett Dam—it's an impressive sight. Despite the abundance of people during the summer, you can still encounter wildlife. Deer are commonly seen grazing in the woods.

Ride Information

Ride Level:	Beginner.
Trail Distances:	Choate Brook Road Loop is 4.7 miles. Old Route 77 Trail is 6.6 miles.
Trail Descriptions:	Paved roads. A few short sections that may be challenging for beginners.
Highlights:	Picnicking, fishing, horseback riding, hiking. Fabulous mountain bike trail network.
Start:	Between Routes 114 and 13, about 5 miles east of Weare. Start trails from the parking lot by the Clough State Park ticket booth.
Note:	The park fee is $2.50 per person. Remember, other vehicles may also be on the trails.

A little friend who'd like to share your picnic lunch.

Ride Options

1. Choate Brook Road Loop. 4.7-mile loop. Head west out of the parking lot. Turn right on the paved road. A sign here says "Service Road Dead End." At .5 mile ride or walk around the yellow gate. At Y, bear right on Old Route 77. The road becomes loose gravel. At 1.9 miles turn left on Choate Brook Road. Go around the orange gate and up the hill. It's now downhill! But be careful—loose rocks and gravel could cause an accident. At Four Corners, turn left on Bassett Mill Road. Some sections of Bassett Mill Road are very sandy. Be careful! At 4 miles you come to an orange gate, then an intersection. Turn here on River Road a very short way, then right on Old Route 77, around the yellow gate and back to the parking lot.

2. Old Route 77 Trail. 6.6 miles out-and-back. Head west out of the parking lot. Turn right on the paved road. A sign here says "Service Road Dead End." At .5 mile ride or walk around the yellow gate. At Y, bear right on Old Route 77. At 1.9 miles you cross over Choate Brook Road, still on Old Route 77. Fifty yards from the intersection, turn right onto a dirt trail. Climb three moderate hills and you'll be at a three-way intersection. Stay on the middle trail marked Stark Pond Loop Trail. At 2.4 miles you cross Mansion road, then at 2.6 miles, you cross Winslow Road. At 3.4 miles turn right at the junction. Immediately take a right on a narrow paved road. At 3.7 miles the trail is obstructed by boulders. Walk around them and bear right onto Winslow Road. Shortly, you'll pass the yellow gate. Note the white paint on the road—it's the high water mark for the flood in April 1987.

At 4.5 miles cross the stone bridge, then bear left at the fork toward the Stark Pond parking lot. Continue on this dirt road through the parking lot and back onto Old Route 77. Return to Clough State Park via Old Route 77.

3. Expanded Trails. Turn to the next chapter for the Hopkinton-Everett Reservoir larger area. (Clough State Park is within the reservoir property.)

CHAPTER 26

HOPKINTON-EVERETT RESERVOIR

"This ain't no place for boys!" That's what the expert rider who researched this ride location said about it. Nor, for that matter, is Hopkinton-Everett Reservoir for anyone who doesn't know what serious mountain biking's all about. So if you're a novice or a Sunday rider, move on. Advanced intermediates and experts, read on.

This is the "expanded version" mentioned in the last chapter—i.e., Hopkinton-Everett Reservoir in Dunbarton and Weare encompasses Clough State Park featured in the previous chapter. The Reservoir is a larger area, covering over 8,000 acres and some of the finest advanced mountain bike riding in the country. Tremendous scenery. Challenging (and sometimes downright dangerous) trails. Wildlife. And unlimited good times!

Hopkinton-Everett's trail system is a cooperative effort of the U.S. Army Corps of Engineers, NH Department of Resources and Economic Development Trails Bureau, and Merrimack Valley Trail Riders. Trails are used by motorized bikes as well as mountain bikes. So be prepared to meet others along the trails. Ride responsibly. Please.

Stay on the gravel roads after a rain to avoid damaging the dirt trails where erosion will occur if torn up and skidded on by fat-tired bikes. Obey all trail closing signs. The area has excellent signage and provides maps at the trailhead, but the network of trails is so vast, you could still get lost.

Hopkinton • Everett Reservoir

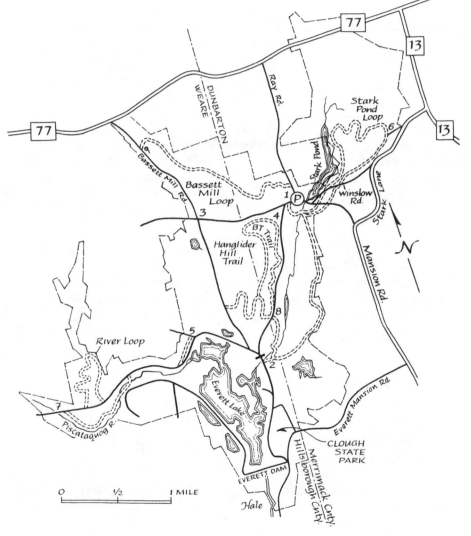

The single-track trails in this Reservoir demand good equipment and advanced bike-handling abilities. All that aside, this area rates a B—for Blast!

Words to the wise: Carry lots and lots of water. Bring a compass. Ride with a friend.

Ride Information

Ride Level: Advanced intermediate to expert.
Trail Distances: Park has 20 miles of trails. Many 3- and 4-mile loops.
Trail Descriptions: Gravel roads. Mostly single track. Muddy in the spring. Roots, rocks. Steep climbs. Tough sledding at times.
Highlights: Fantastic mountain bike network. Tremendous scenery. Wildlife (Early mornings or dusk). For attractions in nearby Concord, refer to Chapter 9.
Start: Take Exit 2 off I-89. Go east on Route 13 to Route 77. Turn left on Route 13 for .7 mile, then right on Winslow Road. Park in the Stark Pond parking area a mile up the road. There's a large map here indicating all the trails.
Note: Buggy in late spring and early summer. Signs indicating "ATVs Prohibited" do not apply to mountain bikes.

Ride Options

For easier communication, some of the trail intersections are numbered on the map.

1. Bassett Mill Loop. A 6.5-mile loop. Expert level. This loop is difficult riding. Ride from the parking lot to area 9, 3 and back to parking lot. There are numerous steep uphills and downhills on this loop. Horseshoe Hill, which you'll recognize by its sign, drops off a shallow ledge, turns abruptly and climbs uphill. Mud, wet areas and brook-crossings present their own challenges. Once you connect with Bassett Mill Road, it will be smoother sledding—it's a well-drained gravel road.

2. Hanglider Hill Trail. A 9.5-mile loop. A black diamond trail. Expert level ride. From parking lot, go to intersection 2, 3 and back to 1 at parking lot. This requires more technical climbing. Lots of uphills, but every uphill in life has its benefit—this one is a panoramic view of the horizon.

3. BT Trail Loop. A 10-mile loop if you include getting there from the parking lot. Very difficult. Starting at the parking lot, go to intersection 2, 8 onto the BT Trail area to 4, and back to 8 and 1.

4. Stark Pond Loop. A 3.5-mile loop. This is the easiest of the trails on this map. But it's still not for the faint of heart. Leave the parking lot. Ride around the number 6 loop area and back to the parking lot. You need agility and skill to navigate this winding, quick-turning trail. A sandy patch at the loop turnaround area may cause you to walk your bike.

5. River Loop. FEO: For Experts Only. Dubbed a double diamond, this loop is extremely difficult and challenging. From intersection 5, travel out to area 7, loop around River Loop and back to 5. If you start this ride from the Stark Pond parking area, it's a looooong ride—about 14.5 miles. If you'd rather do a shorter loop, start from the Clough State parking area—see the map from the previous chapter. That loop, from intersection 2, to 5, 7, loop around, back to 5 and 2, is 8 miles.

CHAPTER 27

BEAR BROOK STATE PARK

Well I hate to disappoint you, but Bear Brook is devoid of bears. Only one has been spotted by the park manager in the 30 years he has been there. So don't be concerned about camping out or running into one in the woods. Although you may not find bears, you will find beaver, moose, plenty of other wildlife and one of the best mountain bike networks in the state.

A huge beaver lodge dominates Bear Hill Pond. A ride or walk around Hayes Marsh is apt to be rewarding, especially in the early morning or evening when the beavers, muskrats and Great Blue Herons are most active.

If you want to combine other activities with your biking plans, a hike up 721-foot Catamount Hill should fit the bill. The trail begins near the toll booth at intersection 31.

With nearly 10,000 acres of parklands, Bear Brook in Allenstown is the largest developed state park in New Hampshire. It has something for everyone. Hiking. Biking. Camping. Swimming. Canoeing. In the winter, cross-country skiing, snowshoeing and snowmobiling.

Or visit the New Hampshire Antique Snowmobile Museum, the Museum of Family Camping, Old Allenstown Meeting House, or the Richard Diehl Civilian Conservation Corps (CCC) Museum. Bear Brook Camp, one of the most complete CCC camps remaining intact in the country, is on the National Register of Historic Places.

Trails seem endless. Over 40 miles of fabulous trails leading to marshes, bogs, summits and ponds, offer many options for mountain bikers, hikers and equestrians.

Ride Information

Ride Level:	All levels.
Trail Distances:	Park has 40+ miles of trails.
Trail Descriptions:	Paved roads have moderate car traffic. Gravel roads are wide and offer great cycling. Single- and double-track trails.
Highlights:	Wildlife. Swimming. Fishing. See beginning information in chapter for more attractions.
Start:	From Hooksett, drive 5 miles north on Route 28 to Bear Brook in Allenstown. Past the toll booth 2 miles is Podunk Road. Park there.
Note:	There is an admission fee charged mid-May through mid-October. Canoe rentals available.
	Remember trails are multi-use. Surrounding property owners have a reputation for being very accommodating to park visitors. Please work to maintain that congeniality by respecting their rights as private property owners.
	Hunting is allowed in the park late fall, so avoid it then.
	It's a good idea to take a copy of this map along to follow the intersections that are marked on the map. It's a very large park and it'll be easier to get around with this map's assistance.

Ride Options

For easier communication, trail intersections areas are numbered on the map. This map will be a bit easier to follow if you photocopy the map and mark the trails with different colored highlighters, so that they stand out on the page. Just follow the numbers!

1. Smith Pond Loop. A 4-mile loop. Novice rider level. A super short ride that incorporates pavement, packed trails, single-track and dirt roads. Its quiet wooded area smells of heavenly pine.

From the parking lot, go to intersection XC5, XC7, XC9 and back to parking lot at intersection 1.

2. Bear Hill Pond Loop. An 8-mile loop. Challenging riding. Begin your ride at the beach (intersection 22) by Beaver Pond, go to intersection 21, 20, 7, 25, 12, 13, 9, 7 and back to the beach at intersection 22.

Bear Hill is a nice ride, but it was appropriately named. It's a bear. And it's a hill. It gets tiring. Hang tough.

3. Dodge Road Loop. A 10-mile loop. Advanced beginner to intermediate. This trail is a wonderful opportunity to just revel in the beauty of the great outdoors. It does get tricky through the marsh. Also pay close

Nothing quite compares to the beauty of the scenic backroads of New Hamsphire.

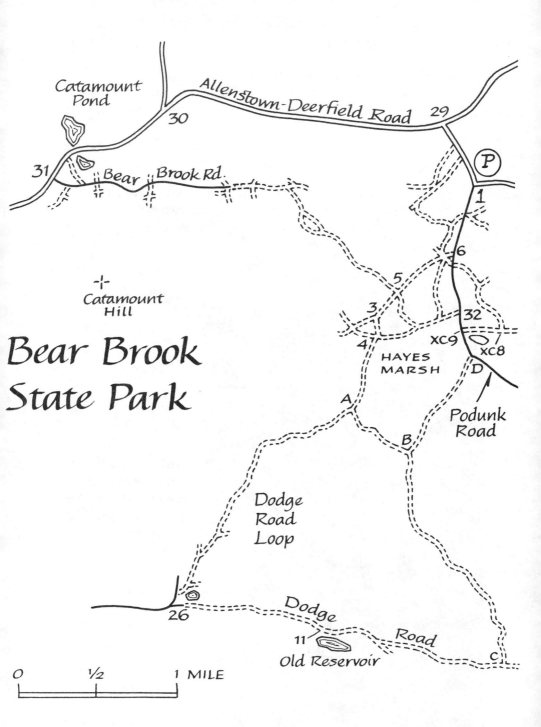

Catamount
Pond

Allenstown-Deerfield Road

30   29

31   Bear   Brook Rd.

P

1

6

5

3   32

Catamount
Hill

4   xC9

xC8

HAYES
MARSH

D

Bear Brook
State Park

A

Podunk
Road

B

Dodge
Road
Loop

26

Dodge

11

Old Reservoir

Road

C

0   ½   1 MILE

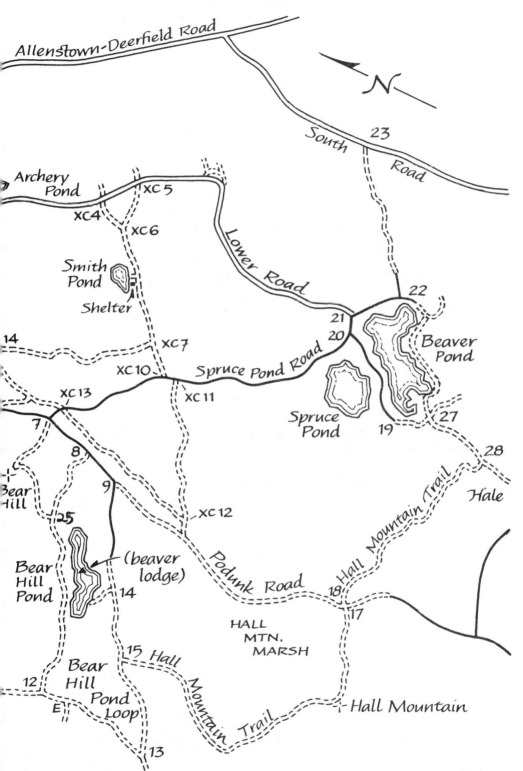

Allenstown-Deerfield Road

South Road 23

N

Archery Pond
XC5
XC4
XC6
Lower Road
Smith Pond
Shelter
22
Beaver Pond
21
20
14
XC7
XC10
Spruce Pond Road
XC13
XC11
Spruce Pond
19
27
7
28
8
Hale
Bear Hill
9
XC12
Hall Mountain Trail
25
Bear Hill Pond
(beaver lodge)
Podunk Road
18
14
17
15 Hall
HALL MTN. MARSH
Bear Hill Pond Loop
12
Mountain Trail
E
Hall Mountain
13

attention to the map and directions or you'll end up on a spur road or two.

From parking lot, go to intersection D, B, then A. Then left until you intersect with Dodge Road at intersection 26. Then to intersection C, B, and D. At intersection 6, you'll find a large open area and a cross-country trail on the right. Follow it to the parking lot. (It's the best trail in the park!)

4. Figure-8 Loop. A 12-mile loop. A good all-around trail loop with a few technical areas. But walk your bike if those areas are uncomfortable. It's a beautiful trail and worth the effort.

From parking lot, ride to XC4 intersection, then to XC10 (Spruce Pond Road). Follow Spruce Pond Road to marker 20, 19 and on to intersection 27. Turn right there to intersection 28. Then pay careful attention for the right turn onto Hall Mountain Trail. At 18 turn right back to parking area at intersection 1.

5. Elongated Figure-8 Loop. A 13.5-mile loop. Advanced riders. This is a trail that requires stamina—and lots of skill. Riding from marker 17 to 15 is the most difficult trail in the park. You may have to carry your bike quite a bit because of trail blockage and rocky conditions. And don't forget the bug spray—the marshes and beaches spawn a healthy mosquito population.

Start your ride at intersection 31, go east on Bear Brook Road. This area is poorly marked. Stay on the wider trail. At intersection 32 (Podunk Road) go right all the way to intersection 17. Right on Hall Mountain Trail, to 15, 9, and left on Podunk Road to intersection 29, where you go left on Allenstown-Deerfield Road and back to the starting point at intersection 31.

6. Boundary Loop. A 20-mile loop. For advanced riders because of the mileage and terrain.

OK guys. This is a marathon ride. Are you ready for it? It's not for the faint of heart. Allow probably three to four hours for this one. Bring plenty of water—and a buddy. You'll have a fabulous time! Here goes.

Start your ride at intersection 31, go east on Bear Brook Road. This area is poorly marked. Stay on the wider trail. At intersection 5, turn right. Ride to intersection 26. Turn left on Dodge Road. Stay on it until marker 13. Then go left to 15, right on Hall Mountain Trail. Cross Podunk Road (still on Hall Mountain Trail), to intersection 28. Left, pass Beaver Pond on your left, to beach at 22. Left again to 21 where you'll take the right fork on Lower Road back to the parking area on Podunk Road. To return to where you began the ride, go right to intersection 29, then left. Take Allenstown-Deerfield Road back to intersection 31.

CHAPTER 28

PAWTUCKAWAY STATE PARK

"P awtuckaway," the Indian name given this park, means "the place of the big buck." Well, in this park you won't see much of the green sort nor of the kind with antlers, but you will see that its vast network of trails is why its earned the reputation for being an excellent destination for mountain biking.

Located in Nottingham, 5,500-acre Pawtuckaway is a popular destination for many reasons. Some people come to see the boulders. Strewn near Round Pond is a random scattering of house-size boulders, thought to be one of the largest fields of glacial erratics in the world. The area is designated as a New Hampshire Natural Area.

Some people head to Pawtuckaway for the beach. The 800-acre lake provides excellent bass and pickerel fishing, canoeing that offers soul-calming solitude, and a swimming beach perfect for a family picnic or a refreshing swim after a bike ride.

Hiking ranks as one of the favorite pastimes in the park. Twenty-five miles of trails and three peaks of the Pawtuckaway Range to climb (North Peak: 995 feet, Middle Peak: 845 feet and South Peak: 885 feet) offers options for mini-treks. From the peaks you can see the Atlantic Ocean and the White Mountains.

Camping is popular, but campsites are limited to 170. But part of the fun is camping on an island. Campers can pitch a tent on Horse Island on the water's edge. Don't worry about stampedes, there are no horses inhabiting the island these days.

Birdwatching enthusiasts come in search of Blackburnian warblers—Neotropical migrants that prefer larger tracts of older-growth forests. They'll also see blue-gray gnat-catchers, goshawks, grouse and turkey vultures.

But let's talk about mountain biking. Pawtuckaway State Park has 15 miles of trails. The terrain is moderately challenging, with some short technical climbs and descents. But all levels of riders can find trails that are well worth including in their day's activities. Marshland along Fundy Trail on the northwestern side of the park, where beaver, deer and Great Blue Heron are often seen early mornings, is an excellent and easy ride. Other areas, such as Shaw Trail are expert level, and call for more advanced riding skills and equipment.

Pawtuckaway State Park is about equidistant between Manchester and Portsmouth. Both cities offer a terrific variety of attractions. For some suggestions for things to see and do in Manchester, check out Chapter 31. For ideas in the Portsmouth area, see Chapter 29.

Ride Information

Ride Level: All levels, but primarily novice and intermediate.

Trail Distances: Park has 15+ miles of trails.

Trail Descriptions: Paved roads, dirt roads, single- and double-track trails. Some technical climbs and descents. In the spring, trails are muddy. Don't tear up the land, respect it. (Some trails may be closed because it's *too* muddy.) Side trails are not well marked.

Highlights: Wildlife. Swimming. Fishing. See beginning information in chapter for more info.

Start: From the Route 101/156 intersection in Raymond, drive 3.5 miles north on Route 156 to park entrance. Several parking areas are noted on map.

Note: There is an admission fee charged mid-May through mid-October. But mountain bikers are permitted to ride in the park year-round. There are three other ways to enter the park without a fee. See map. Remember trails are multi-use. You may encounter hikers and horse-back riders.
Summer hatches a fair amount of mosquitoes. Take bug juice.

Boulder field

1011' North Mtn.

107

Power Lines

South Ridge

11

Round Pond Rd.

MIDDLE MTN. LOOP

Middle Mtn.

7

800'

15

P

6

Reservation Road

12

Tower Rd.

P

13

South Mtn 908'

14

Lookout Tower

5 Mountain Trail

Mountain Trail

Pawtuckaway
State Park

0   ½   1 MILE

156

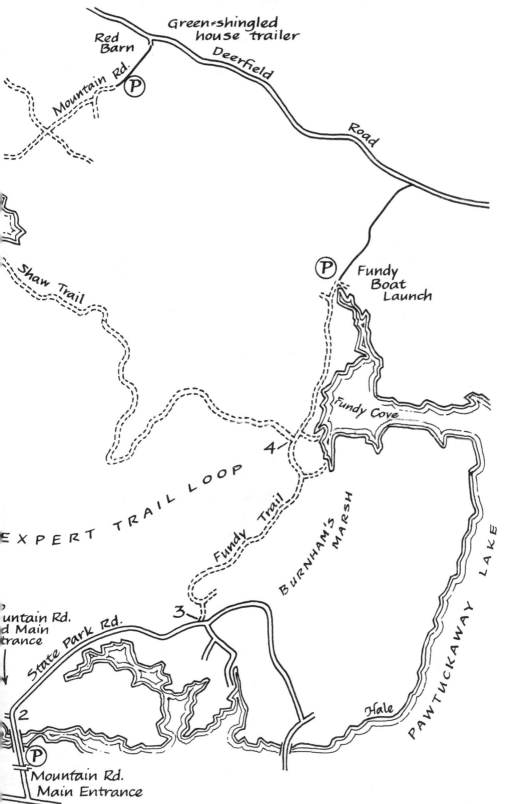

Red Barn

Green-shingled house trailer

Mountain Rd.

Deerfield

Road

Shaw Trail

Fundy Boat Launch

Fundy Cove

EXPERT TRAIL LOOP

Fundy Trail

4

BURNHAM'S MARSH

PAWTUCKAWAY LAKE

untain Rd.
d Main
trance

State Park Rd.

3

Hale

2

Mountain Rd.
Main Entrance

Ride Options

For easier communication, trail intersections are numbered on the map. This map will be a bit easier to follow if you photocopy it and mark the trails with different colored highlighters, and then, just follow the numbers!

Some background on some of the roads that are available for riding:

Fundy Trail. This 1.5-mile stretch offers excellent mountain biking. This is the easiest biking trail in the park. The trail runs from the boat launch off Deerfield Road to the toll road near the camping areas.

South Ridge Trail. From intersection 9 to 8 is all uphill. Lots of switchbacks that climbs up to a ridge. A single-track trail that is a definite expert level.

Shaw Trail. Very difficult 3-mile trail. This very challenging trail begs the rider to know what technical means when it comes to mountain biking. If that's a mystery to you, stay off it. Lots of rocks, tough climbs and erosion indicate this ain't for baby bikers.

• • •

1. Middle Mountain Loop. A 5.6-mile loop. Novice level. This ride is particularly breathtaking during foliage season. The oak and hemlock forest along the ponds and bogs unveil outstanding natural beauty. In spring, wildflowers scatter the pond edge and invite photo opportunities.

Start from Route 107 and park under the power lines. Take Reservation Road to 14 counter clockwise to 11, back to 13, and right on Reservation Road back to your car.

This ride has easy, moderate climbs, made more difficult due to loose gravel, washouts and loose sands. At times, it is necessary to get off your bike to negotiate the sandy areas or handle an uphill climb. But all in all, it's a moderate up-and-down trail with short, easy climbs.

In one section along Round Pond Road with ponds on both sides of you, it could be quite muddy early in the spring—because of rain and beavers damming it.

2. Middle Mountain Road Addition 1. You can extend the previous ride in a couple of ways. At intersection 11, you can take a right and ride to Round Pond, a beautiful, remote, wilderness pond. Use caution as the road has washouts, loose gravel, rocks, sand, and is mostly down hill to the pond, which obviously will require some uphill riding on the way back. This adds 2.2 miles to your ride.

3. Middle Mountain Road Addition 2. Another extension to ride one is after your left turn onto Tower Road, take a right at intersection 6. **Note:** This is not the summit trail, but a trail to the right. Take this trail for a nice .5-mile downhill ride back to the intersection of South Mountain Trail. **Caution:** There are a couple of steep 30-foot sections as well as two fallen logs across this trail. At this Mountain Trail (marked intersection), take a right (not marked). There, a grassy opening in the woods and a single-track trail will take you .1-mile back out to Tower Road. (If you bear left, you will remain on Mountain Trail and be headed 3.0 miles back to the toll road/main entrance.) This extension will add .6 miles to your ride.

4. Mountain Road Trail. A 5-mile in-and-back round trip. Intermediate level or a novice who wants to walk a lot. This trail, which begins off Deerfield Road, starts off easy and fun, but quickly becomes difficult. This ride climbs steadily, with many roots and rocks exposed because of much use. The many years of hiking and biking the trail has endured is evident in the erosion of the land.

The ride in requires many walks uphill because of rocks and roots in the way. The trail is not recommended during the wet season as roots would be slippery and dangerous.

5. Expert Trail Loop. For the expert rider in excellent condition, this is a challenging loop. Combine Shaw Trail, Fundy Trail, Mountain Trail, and Tower Road Trail for an 8-plus mile loop, depending on which loop you ride out.

6. Other Trails. Off the dirt road, a maze of other unmarked roads exist. Many are snowmobile trails in the winter, and all are fun to explore. Do it safely.

CHAPTER 29

ODIORNE POINT STATE PARK

Scottish fishermen landed at Odiorne Point in 1623 and created the first European settlement in New Hampshire. A U.S. Army military base was built on this point to protect Portsmouth Harbor from possible attack during WWII. And today it's open to the public for a variety of activities, including biking.

Odiorne Point State Park proves that easy riding doesn't have to be boring. The 327-acre site on New Hampshire's seacoast in Rye, hosts a network of flat, mostly wide, single-track trails and a paved bicycle path. The park is small enough so that you won't get lost, but big enough to make you wonder if you might be.

Odiorne is a place to bring children, timid friends or reluctant significant others for a first venture off roads. The odds are good they'll emerge with a smile and without a scratch.

If there's more to life than riding, you can find some of it here—a spectacular shoreline with the Isles of Shoals six miles in the distance, picnicking, a boat launch, WWII bunkers, and the Seacoast Science Center, which offers sea-life exhibits, local history and nature walks.

History imposes as you enter the park, a hulking mound of earth at the edge of the parking lot. During WWII, this summer resort area underwent an ambience change as it became Fort Dearborn. Homes were razed and giant concrete bunkers were constructed. One of these overwhelming structures stands just beyond the Seacoast Science Center.

The center, which is managed by New Hampshire Audubon Society, hosts thousands of school children each year.

Tidepooling along the last stretch of undeveloped coastline in New Hampshire is a fun adventure. One of the center's naturalists adds color to the event with lots of information. Take a short ride or walk to the salt marsh at the northern end of the park and watch the herons, egrets, and shorebirds—sandpipers, plovers, terns and lesser yellowlegs—all love this area during low tide. Other wildlife call Odiorne Point State Park home. You may encounter deer and a multitude of rabbits on the trails in this park.

The curious can touch and learn about tidepool animals in the indoor touch-tank, watch deep ocean fish swim in the 1,000-gallon Gulf of Maine tank, and follow nearly four centuries of local history on a walk-through-time exhibit. The center also has a Nature Store, where specially selected marine-related gifts, books and educational items are for sale. The center is open daily year-round.

So, the area has much to do. But back to biking. You'll find little in the way of technical challenges in this park. High speeds will lead to too-close encounters with horrified pedestrians. Make a day of it. Take a gentle ride. Fire up the coals for a cookout. Dive into the waves at nearby Wallis Sands Beach. But if that's not enough, there's plenty to do in the Seacoast area of New Hampshire.

Only 18 winding miles of seacoast exist in New Hampshire, but the area is a treasure trove of history and culture. Historic homes. Fascinating museums. Fabulous restaurants. Professional theater. Public gardens. Antique shops. Art galleries. Factory outlets. Great fishing. It's all here on the Seacoast of New Hampshire.

Following are a smattering of the many attractions available while you're in the Seacoast area.

Strawbery Banke Museum

Located on their original sites in Portsmouth, the more than 42 historic buildings known as Strawbery Banke, reflect four centuries of architectural and social change in one of America's oldest neighborhoods. Enjoy costumed role players, the gardens, exhibits, furnished houses, craft demonstrations and historical re-enactments. A museum restau-

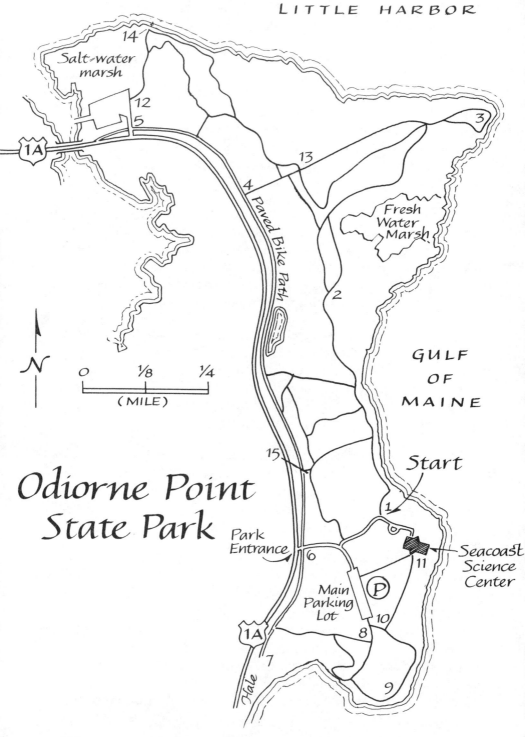

LITTLE HARBOR

14

Salt-water marsh

12

5

1A

13

4

Paved Bike Path

3

Fresh Water Marsh

2

N

0   ⅛   ¼

(MILE)

GULF OF MAINE

15

Start

1

Odiorne Point State Park

Park Entrance

6

Seacoast Science Center

11

P

Main Parking Lot

10

1A

8

7

Hale

9

rant and gift shops are also available. Open May to November. Call 603 433-1100, for additional information.

Great Bay National Estuarine Research Reserve

In Durham, this estuary comprises 4,471 acres of tidal waters and mud flats and 48 miles of shoreline on an Atlantic bay. The range of environments in the estuary include salt marsh, tidal creeks, woodlands and open fields. Great Bay estuary is the haunt of seabirds, migrating land birds, herons and harbor seals. The early morning hours are the best time to appreciate the area. Its isolation from populated centers nearby brings out the Thoreau in all of us.

Direct access to the property is at Adams Point in Durham, with water access via Little Bay and the Piscataqua River. Call 603 868-1095 with questions.

Portsmouth Historic Houses

What is now Portsmouth was first settled in 1630. First called Piscataqua after the river which forms its eastern border, it was soon renamed "Strawbery Banke" after a field of wild strawberries. Finally the town became Portsmouth in 1653. A historic area of the port city boasts a wealth of wonderful colonial homes. Admission fees are charged to tour these homes.

Visit Jackson House, circa 1664, the oldest house in New Hampshire and one of the earliest examples of plank-frame construction in New England.

Rundlet-May House is a superb mansion built in 1807 by self-made merchant James Rundlet. Period furnishings, Rumford roasting oven and original landscaping offers hours of interesting exploration.

John Paul Jones House shows off a fine collection of china, colonial furniture and elegant gardens. Tours by costumed guides are provided Memorial Day to mid-October.

Merchant, patriot and governor John Langdon built his home in the late 1700s. The Governor John Langdon house is known for its formal garden.

Moffatt-Ladd House and Warner House are a couple of other choices for historic home tours. While the Moffatt-Ladd House lays claim to a secret underground passage, Warner House is New England's finest example of an urban brick 18th century mansion containing splendid interior decorations and a fine collection of furnishings.

Nearby Exeter also has its share of historic colonial homes.

Sandown Old Meeting House

Credited by many as the finest meeting house in New Hampshire, the Sandown Old Meeting House (circa 1774), is considered by some the finest in America. Historians have lavish praise for its purity of design. Its excellent example of the skill of colonial craftspeople has earned it a place on the National Register of Historic Buildings. In its original condition, the building showcases box pews, slave pews, paupers benches and a wine glass pulpit. Call 603 887-3453.

Fuller Gardens

At Fuller Gardens are two acres of estate flower gardens, circa 1939, where 1,500 rose bushes bloom all summer. Also on the grounds are perennials, Japanese gardens and a conservatory. Open May through October. Call 603 964-5414 for additional information.

Odiorne Point offers not only great biking, but magnificent ocean views as well.

USS Albacore

The Port of Portsmouth Maritime Museum in Albacore Park is home of the USS Albacore. Built in 1953, it is a prototype and testing submarine for the U.S. Navy. A film and tour show visitors how the 55-man crew lived and worked aboard the vessel. There is an admission fee. For additional information, call 603 436-3680.

Isles of Shoals

The Isles of Shoals is an archipelago of nine islands (eight at high tide) in the Atlantic, an hour from Portsmouth, that was one of the major attractions for new settlers. The islands were named for the shoals (schools) of fish that supposedly jumped into the nets of fishermen.

In the 19th century the islands were an offshore retreat for the literary and art crowd. Now cruises take visitors to the island for picnics and hiking. Whale-watch expeditions and mini-voyages are conducted by the Isles of Shoals Steamship Company with ghost and pirate stories in abundance. You can reach the Isles of Shoals Steamship Company to inquire about cruises at 603 431-5000 or 800 441-4620.

For even more information on the attractions on New Hampshire's Seacoast, contact the New Hampshire Department of Resources and Economic Development, the Seacoast Council on Tourism (603 436-7678 or outside New Hampshire: 800 221-5623), or the Portsmouth Chamber of Commerce at 603 436-1118.

Ride Information

Ride Level:	Beginner and intermediate.
Trail Distances:	Park has 4-5 miles of trails.
Trail Descriptions:	Paved roads, dirt roads, single-track trails. Flat.
Highlights:	Wildlife. Picnicking. Seacoast Science Center. See information in chapter for nearby attractions.
Start:	Take the main entrance to Odiorne State Park, just off Route 1A in Rye.
Note:	There is an admission fee charged. Trails are multi-use. You may encounter pedestrians. The WWII bunkers and the jetty at Frost Point are off-limits to visitors.

Ride Options

For easier communication, trail areas are numbered on the map. There are no numbered area markers in the park. Odiorne Point State Park is a fun place to ride. It's a relatively small park with a web of trails to ride on. You can ride it all in an hour with no chance of getting lost. You don't really need loop suggestions, but we'll provide one and then you can create the rest on your own.

1. North Loop. A 2.2-mile loop. Novice level. From the main parking lot, head to the beginning of the trail on the far side of the bunker at area marker 1. Travel to area marker 3 at Frost Point.

At the jetty, take in the view of the Atlantic Ocean and Little Harbor. Then head west on the wide trail past the bunker at area 13 where you'll take a right onto a single-track trail. Pass over a 10-foot hump and merge with the trail coming from the left. Continue on to intersection 14. Then on to 12, 5, 15 and back to where you began at intersection 1.

2. Other Trails. The playground area is south of the parking lot should you want to stop for a time with kids. Don't miss the Dolphin Fountain on a trail near intersection 15.

CHAPTER 30

LITCHFIELD STATE FOREST

Famous German-born American architect, Ludwig Mies van der Rohe, coined the phrase "Less is more." He believed there is elegance and beauty in simple things. This concept is transferable to the tiny forest in the Merrimack Valley Region of New Hampshire, Litchfield State Forest. It's not well known. It's not a large area. It's not teeming with crowds of people. Nevertheless, there is beauty in its simplicity.

Litchfield State Forest, a small 330-acre area located in the town of Litchfield, is equidistant from Manchester and Nashua. It's truly a paradise for mountain bikers. Pine-needle covered trails. Quiet woods. Heavenly pine scent. Flat. It's perfect for a Sunday ride with the family or a quick run for exercise after work.

If this isn't enough riding, check out nearby Pawtuckaway State Park or the Rockingham Recreation Trail. Both are described in this book.

Litchfield State Forest's convenient location in southern New Hampshire invites other opportunities for exploration off your bike. If you want to make a day or weekend trip of your adventure, here are some suggestions for other activities in New Hampshire's Merrimack Valley Region.

Robert Frost Farm

"The Road Less Traveled" and other famous Robert Frost poems were inspired by Frost's time spent on his farm in Derry. He lived there

from 1901 to 1909. The simple, two-story white clapboard structure is typical of 1880s New England architecture. This national historic landmark features guided tours, period furnishings, nature-poetry interpretive trails through fields and woodlands. For more information, call 603 432-3091.

America's Stonehenge

America's Stonehenge is one of the largest and possibly the oldest megalithic (stone-constructed) sites in North America. Located in north Salem, it has long presented an intriguing puzzle to archeologists, astronomers and historians. Like England's Stonehenge, it was built by ancient people well-versed in astronomy and stone construction. It was and still can be used to determine specific solar and lunar events of the year.

Archeological excavation at the site has uncovered numerous historic and prehistoric artifacts. From these, researchers have narrowed the possibilities down to Native American culture or a migrant European population. As yet, no single theory has been proven, but research continues on this oldest-of-human-created rock structures in the U.S. For additional information and hours, call 603 893-8300.

Anheuser-Busch Brewery and its Clydesdale Horses

In an hour-long tour at the Anheuser-Busch Brewery in Merrimack, you can learn about the 100-year-old Anheuser-Busch's slow, natural brewing process and have a chance to see the legendary Budweiser Clydesdales up close. The tour is highlighted by historical displays and Anheuser-Busch memorabilia that explains the stages of its progress to becoming the world's largest brewer.

The Budweiser-Clydesdale Hamlet and the Anheuser-Busch Tour Center are classic examples of European architecture. The award-winning landscaping and gardens alone are worth the trip. No charge for the tour. Gift shop. For more information, call 603 595-1202.

Panda Children's Museum

If you have younger children that you're just introducing to biking and would like other activities to combine with your mountain-biking adventure, check out the Panda Children's Museum in nearby Goffstown.

PASSACONWAY
COUNTRY CLUB

3A

Litchfield
State Forest

N

Hillcrest Road

Albuquerque Road

P

LITCHFIELD

STATE

FOREST

Brenton Street

0   1/8 MILE

153

Children can experiment with different musical instruments, become a builder, learn about other cultures, play in the jungle room, explore the interactive computers and explore the world of medicine. The museum also has a large playground and petting zoo (seasonal). Call for rates and hours at 603 623-6660.

For even more information on the attractions in New Hampshire's Merrimack Valley region, contact the New Hampshire Department of Resources and Economic Development at 603 271-2343, and request a copy of *The Official New Hampshire Guidebook*. Or write for a free copy from New Hampshire Office of Travel and Tourism, Box 1856, Concord, NH 03302-1856.

Ride Information

Ride Level:	Beginner and intermediate.
Trail Distances:	Forest has 4-5 miles of trails. Plus other town gravel roads to explore.
Trail Descriptions:	Paved roads, dirt roads, single-track trails. Flat.
Highlights:	Quiet. Easy cycling. See information in chapter for nearby attractions.
Start:	On Route 3A heading south in Litchfield, across from the Passaconway Golf Course, go east (left) on Hillcrest Road for .6 mile to the Litchfield State Forest sign. Left on Albuquerque Dr. Park on the right.
Note:	There is no admission fee charged. Signs indicate "Wheel Vehicles Prohibited." It applies to motorized vehicles, not mountain bikes.

Ride Options

Litchfield State Forest is a small park with a web of trails to ride on. You can probably ride them all in an hour. You don't really need loop suggestions, because the map is simple and self-explanatory. But here are just a few ride thoughts.

1. West-East Out-and-Back Trail. A 2.4-mile round trip. Novice level. From the main entrance by the boulders, head out on the trail for 1.4

miles to the end and back. Along the way are several spur roads that you can explore.

2. Other Trails. If you ride half a mile farther down on Albuquerque Road, there's a gated gravel road. Take a right here. The road connects with Brenton Street. But on the right is another wide gravel road. Go for it.

CHAPTER 31

ROCKINGHAM RECREATIONAL TRAIL

"It ain't over 'til it's over." Well, this trail is best considered a work in progress. Rockingham Recreational Trail is a triangular-shaped trail that is primarily reclaimed railroad bed. The New Hampshire State Trails system is to be commended for the work done on this trail so far. It is a super trail now, but when it's finally finished, it will be outstanding.

The triangle begins at Massabesic Lake in Auburn (immediately east of Manchester on Bypass 28), travels east to Epping. From Epping, you travel south west to Windham Depot and then back to Massabesic Lake. Parts of this triangle are well-maintained, easy pedaling, scenic areas. Other parts are more challenging.

The Rockingham Rec Trail has three distinct legs. Each leg is 15 to 20 miles long (roughly 54 miles total). The riding grade is mostly flat cinder and gravel terrain. Some stretches of the trail are smooth and firm. Some feature undulations and loose gravel.

The Rockingham Rec Trail's convenient location in southern New Hampshire also invites other opportunities for exploration *off* your bike.

See Chapter 9 and 30 for additional ideas. Or for scads of other suggestions, pick up a copy of *The Official New Hampshire Guidebook* at state information centers along I-93, write the New Hampshire Office of Travel and Tourism at Box 1856, Concord, NH 03302-1856, or call the New Hampshire Office of Travel and Tourism at 603 271-2343 and request a free copy.

If you want to make a day or weekend trip of your adventure, here are some suggestions for other activities nearby.

Currier Gallery of Art

One of the finest small museums in the country, Currier Gallery of Art in Manchester is a treasure waiting to be discovered. Recognized internationally for its collection on American fine and decorative arts, the Currier features a permanent collection of paintings and sculpture by American and European masters that spans the 13th-20th centuries. The museum also owns and operates the Zimmerman House, a 1950 Usonian home designed by architect Frank Lloyd Wright. A fee is charged. Call for information at 603 669-6144.

Canobie Lake Park

First opened in 1902 as a street railway amusement park, Canobie Lake in Salem is still a favorite destination for families. Today the antique carousel with hand-carved horses dating back to the 1890s, authentic 24 gauge steam train and paddlewheel riverboat are reminiscent of days gone by. Traditional themes and high-tech thrills combine for entertainment for all ages. You can choose from rides, games, shows, arcades, lake cruises, dining, flower gardens and tree-lined promenades. For price, hours and other information, call 603 893-3506.

Amoskeag Fishways

It's a ritual older than civilization, one of nature's magnificent mysteries. Every springtime the salmon of the Atlantic respond to a silent calling, and start a grueling swim upstream, to return to the fresh waters of their births. You can see it while it's happening for just a few mad weeks during springtime at the Amoskeag Fishways in Manchester.

You can actually go beneath the surface of the Merrimack River to watch this ritual firsthand. Open daily May and June when several species of fish return to spawn. In addition to the viewing window, the fishways features a historic diorama, waterpower displays, an audiovisual show and guided tours. No admission fee.

Stonyfield Farm Yogurt

Meet the folks at the Stonyfield Farm Yogurt Works in North Londonderry and see how yogurts are made. Visitors can tour the yogurt works, traveling from the tropical incubator to the arctic coolers. You can "adopt-a-cow." You also get a free sample of frozen yogurt

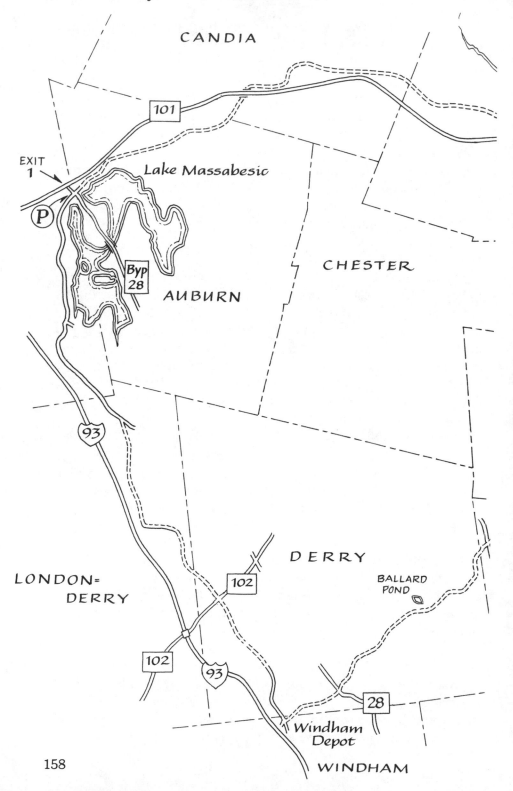

CANDIA

101

EXIT
1

P

Lake Massabesic

Byp
28

AUBURN

CHESTER

93

DERRY

102

BALLARD
POND

LONDON=
DERRY

102

93

28

Windham
Depot

WINDHAM

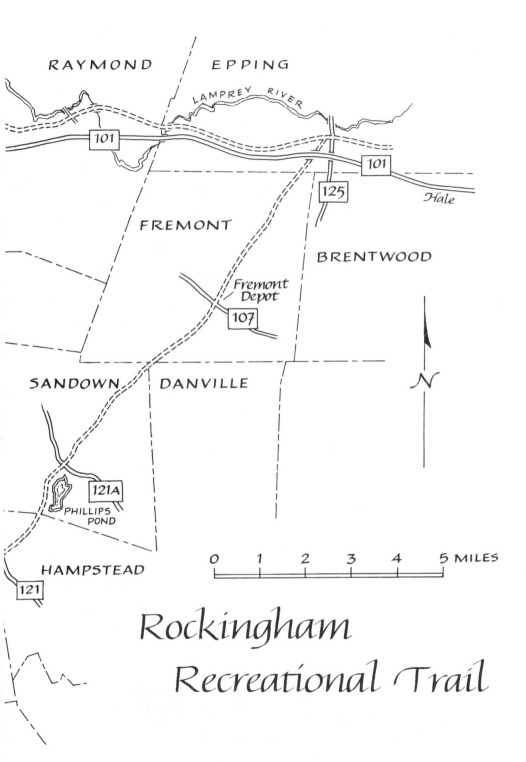

RAYMOND / EPPING

LAMPREY RIVER

101

101

Hale

125

FREMONT

BRENTWOOD

Fremont
Depot

107

N

SANDOWN DANVILLE

121A

PHILLIPS
POND

0 1 2 3 4 5 MILES

HAMPSTEAD

121

Rockingham
Recreational Trail

and cruise the gift shop. Hours vary. Please call for times at 603 437-4040.

Ride Information

Ride Level:	All levels. The first leg is more appropriate for beginners. Legs 2 and 3 are more technical in spots.
Trail Distances:	Each leg is 15-20 miles one way. If you do the entire triangle, it's approximately 54 miles.
Trail Descriptions:	Reclaimed railroad bed. Some dirt trails. Some loose gravel. Some paved. See individual legs for details.
Highlights:	Easy cycling. Scenic. Areas for picnics. Wildlife. See information in chapter for nearby attractions.
Start:	Lake Massabesic parking lot in Auburn. It's at the traffic circle of Route 101 (exit 1) and Bypass 28. Free parking in park. Picnic tables and portable toilets are here. Lake Massabesic is Manchester's drinking water, so no wading or swimming is allowed.
Note:	There is no admission fee charged. The second leg of this ride is shared with other vehicles and occasional walkers. Stay alert.

Ride Options

Rockingham Recreational Trail can be accessed at many points. You can also start the ride at any juncture where two legs of a ride meet. But for our purposes, the description of the trails will be by each leg. This trail is generally outlined on the map, so you need to play close attention to the written route notes.

1. First Leg: Lake Massabesic to Epping
Overview:

This leg is well-groomed and is excellent for riders of all skill levels. It is about 19 miles of flat, easy riding on cinder and packed gravel. Powered vehicles other than snowmobiles are prohibited which keeps the surface in excellent condition. The scenic stretch of this triangle offers wetlands, ponds and wildlife. Many logical turnaround points exist, and numerous places to stop for a picnic. Beginners will not be intimidated. Expert riders will appreciate that they can move along at a brisk pace.

This trail is similar to the Cape Cod railroad bed trail— in short, it's terrific and highly recommended.

Route Notes: First Leg

The trail is a few feet north of the parking area at Massabesic Lake. The old Boston & Maine railroad bed is now periodically identified as the Rockingham Recreational Trail.

Reclaimed railroad beds make for fine riding.

The trail leads east roughly parallel to Route 101 to Newfields. (These route notes will take you only as far as Epping Depot.) The path is virtually unused, except for the area within 5 miles of Massabesic Lake.

The first 5 miles meander through wetlands and ponds, with Massabesic Lake to the immediate south. At 4.6 miles you cross under Route 101 through a culvert with a new wooden floor for safety. There is a rise going up to the culvert that the more experience biker can cruise up and then go through the culvert. Lesser-experienced riders may want to walk their bikes. Soon another culvert appears. Just after the East Candia depot a particularly attractive wetland appears. Lots of birds and small game scurry about.

From the depot, you must get on town roads as the gates are closed to continue on the railroad track trail. You'll need to ride on town roads to get around the closed section. Here's how to do it. Just past the East Candia Railroad depot turn left on Depot Road a short way to T. Turn right on Langford Road. When you're near Route 101, go right on Onway Lake Road. Then turn left on Old Manchester Road for .6 mile and get back on the railroad bed (a right off Old Manchester Road).

At about 12.5 miles you cross the main street of Raymond. This is a good place to stop for a bite to eat or a juice, as several restaurants and convenience stores are available. The Raymond depot building is also the home of the Raymond Historical Society. If you enjoy local colonial town history, stop in.

Just east of Raymond you come to a bridge. The planks are a bit spread apart and tricky to ride across. You could have an accident. The best thing to do is walk your bike.

Soon you pick up the Lamprey River. The Lamprey River is rumored to have excellent fishing. (Carry a pack rod with you if that's of interest.) Parallel the river most of the rest of the way to Epping, the end of the first leg. You finish in the business district of Epping near the Route 125 exit off Route 101.

2. Second Leg: Epping to Windham
Overview:
This leg is more difficult. The trail is still being worked on by the state. While the terrain is flat, it is used by motorized recreation vehicles, which translates into loose gravel and undulations in the path

The state is planning to build an underpass at Route 101, as well as improve the general condition of the trail. Perhaps by the time you read this, it will be a reality. Until it's a reality, we go to plan 2.

Route Notes: Second Leg

It is illegal to cross Route 101 by staying on the railroad bed. So we must use town roads. So plan 2 dictates that we follow the railroad bed parallel to Route 101. When it intersects with Jenness Road (which becomes Fremont Street), go right and travel Fremont Street until it intersects with Martin Road. Go right on Martin Road across Route 101 for .7 mile to the Boston and Main Railroad bed on your right.

Travel on to Fremont Depot at Route 107.

This section has overhanging beech and birch trees, which make for spectacular fall riding. This trail is used by recreation vehicles, so you'll encounter some loose gravel and undulations. But for the most part it's an OK trail.

Cross Route 107 at Fremont and re-enter the trail system through a small park with a baseball field. The trail is clearly marked. Travel another 14 miles to Windham Depot. This last section of leg two has more loose gravel and rolling areas. Expect mud and some water in the spring.

The trail cuts through wetlands almost continuously with a few nice ponds en route. You'll see Ballard Pond about 5 miles before Windham Depot. (Your odometer will read approximately 13.5 miles from Epping.) It's an attractive pond with abounding wildlife and plant life. It's good for fishing, too, especially for smallmouth bass and pickerel.

The remaining part of the trail has more wetlands. It also has loose gravel that's hard to navigate through. You finish this second leg of the triangle at the Windham Public Works gravel pit on Windham Depot Road.

If you started at Massabesic Lake, you're 38 miles into the ride with only 15 miles to go!

3. Third Leg: Windham to Massabesic Lake
Overview:

This leg is half on rail bed and half on the road. The rail bed merges into an active line, so you need to finish the ride on the road. The rail bed is in pretty good shape, but primitive with some rough sections that require caution. Some patches of loose gravel also complicate your ride. This leg of the ride is more urban and less scenic, going directly through downtown Derry and through the suburbs of Manchester. The leg finishes on a short dirt trail back to the Lake Massabesic parking lot.

Route Notes: Third Leg

To begin the third leg, go directly across the Windham Depot Road and follow the orange telephone markings. The first 2 miles are easy riding, although the trail is not particularly scenic. At the 2-mile point you will cross under a road through a culvert and continue to another road shortly after. Cross this road and look for the trail with the orange markers. Don't follow the wider gravel road to the left of the railroad bed. In another mile you bike past a few apartment complexes to the main street (Route 102) of Derry.

Cross 102 and go right for about 100 yards to a road which looks like a driveway to a small shopping center. Follow that entry a few hundred yards to a road that goes up a small hill, crosses a road and descends into Hood Park, which consists of a small pond and recreation area. The bike trail is to the left of the pond, marked by a gate. In .3 mile, you come to a road. Cross that road to a culvert that continues the trail. This culvert has no wooden flooring, so you should walk the bike through it.

The next half mile is rough and slightly confusing as a few trails merge. Follow the orange AT&T markers and use caution on the hills, as they are rough. In approximately another half mile (1.5 miles from Hood Pond), you will cross Route 28. The trail parallels Route 28 for another 1.5 miles to a point where Independence and Auburn Roads come together just before I-93 exit 5. At this point you should leave the trail and follow roads back to Lake Massabesic. (You could go a few more miles on the trail, but it is uninteresting and soon merges into a live railroad line.)

Turn right on Auburn Road for .3 miles to a left on Wilson Road. Follow Wilson Road (a quiet residential road) for a mile to a stop sign where Wilson Road ends. Turn left on Bodwell Road for two miles to the intersection of Hermit Road and Cohas Road with Bodwell Road. Take Cohas Road one mile to a right on Burkett Road, then .3 mile to a right on Island Pond Road.

Island Pond Road soon bears left and becomes Lake Shore Road. At this point, the land to the right (east) is all Manchester Water Works property and all travel on it is prohibited. You'll see the "No Trespassing" signs. You will be on Lake Shore Road for approximately 3 miles. You'll climb several hills. Half a mile past the Manchester Water Works building, the trail reappears. Follow the trail back to the Lake Massabesic parking lot.

CHAPTER 32

PISGAH STATE PARK

The largest property in the New Hampshire state park system, 21-square mile, 13,500-acre Pisgah State Park spans three Monadnock Region towns—Winchester, Chesterfield and Hinsdale. The park protects seven ponds, four highland ridges and numerous wetlands. It's a popular destination for a variety of activities. Canoeists seek out Fullam Pond for its northern wilderness-like remoteness. Hikers explore the maze of hiking trails and climb to the top of Mount Pisgah. ATV enthusiasts also enjoy Pisgah, or Pisgy as the locals call it, for a challenging ride.

If you appreciate history, you can meander about old cemeteries, explore the "technology" used to build old cellarholes, and imagine what it was like to live in the old homesteads back then. The community has long-since deserted these homesites and only remnants of the past remain. Signs beside the road mark the homesites of a number of colonial inhabitants. The foundation of a cider mill built around 1800 is another landmark. It is still surrounded by ancient apple trees. Weathered stone walls stretch through the woods for miles and mark an important route for settlers who arrived in the late 1700s to build homes and clear the land.

Mountain bikers are welcomed on the park's gravel roads and woods roads, but not on the hiking trails. The park is well-kept by the Friends of Pisgah (P.O. Box 1179, Keene, NH 03431), a community group dedicated to helping the park managers maintain the trails. The organization also coordinates adventure outings throughout the year. The park's trail intersections are numbered, making the map easier to understand. Signs at trailheads that read "Wheeled Vehicles Prohibited," *do* refer to bicyclists. So please respect the request. It will assure that mountain bikers will be welcome in the future.

Pisgah State Park's convenient location in the Monadnock Region of New Hampshire invites other opportunities for exploration *off* your bike. For 200-pages of ideas and attractions in New Hampshire, pick up a copy of *The Official New Hampshire Guidebook* at state information centers along I-93, write the New Hampshire Office of Travel and Tourism at Box 1856, Concord, NH 03302-1856, or call the New Hampshire Office of Travel and Tourism at 603 271-2343 to request your free copy.

Ride Information

Ride Level: Intermediate and expert.

Trail Distances: Varied. Options include an 8- and 15-mile loop.

Trail Descriptions: More technical riding. Wet areas, bony, rock outcroppings, loose rocks. Muddy in the spring. Moderate climbing and descending on single- and double-track trails.

Highlights: Wildlife. Beaver ponds. Swimming areas. Remote wilderness.

Start: There are four parking areas in the park. (See map.) We'll take you to the lot off Route 63. From Route 9, turn south on Route 63. In Chesterfield, between the town hall and school, turn left on Old Chesterfield Road. Follow the signs for Pisgah State Park. After .2-mile, turn right on Horseshoe Road. Another 1.6 miles finds you in the parking lot. Information and maps are available here.

Note: There is no admission fee charged.
Park opens officially mid-May.
Stay away during hunting season.
Mosquitoes can be vicious late spring and summer.

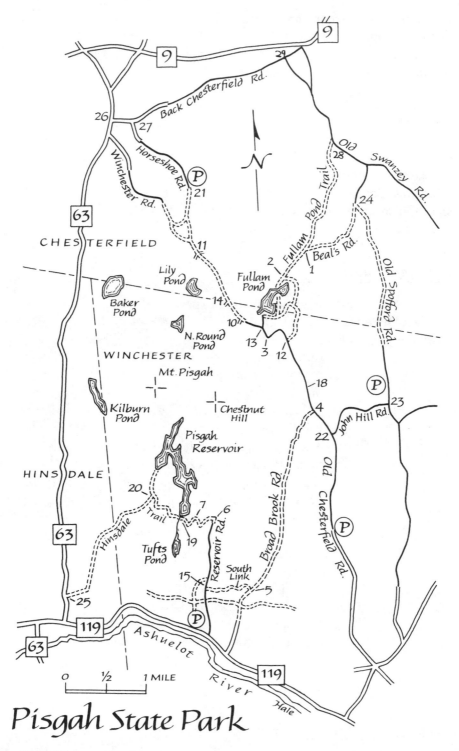

Pisgah State Park

Ride Options

Intersection numbers have been included on the map to make it easier to communicate turns, etc.

1. Fullam Pond Loop. A short easy ride, leave the parking lot at intersection 21 and ride 2.5 miles where you turn left to Fullam Pond. You can ride around several trails adjacent to the pond and travel on to intersection 28, 29, 27 and back to the parking lot at 21.

2. Old Spofford Road Loop. A 15-mile loop. This is a relatively easy ride. You may encounter flooding during the spring. From the parking lot at intersection 21, go to 22, 23, 24, 13 and back to the parking lot at intersection 21.

3. Broad Brook Road Loop. This 27-mile loop is manageable— nearly half of it will be on paved Route 63. Start at the parking lot at intersection 21, go to intersection 4, 5, 15, 6, 20, 25, 26, 27 and back to 21.

You'll enjoy the scenery along this trail. Beaver ponds, wetland animals, and birch and beech tree stands. The trail does get tricky for awhile after intersection 10, and climbs until intersection 4. On your way, Fullam Pond is worth a rest stop. Tall pines line the shoreline and invite a picnic.

You'll turn right on Broad Brook Road, an old wagon trail with a rough surface.

A right on South Link Road makes for easy cycling to Reservoir Road. Reservoir Road is a gravel road that climbs steeply out of the valley and then you enjoy the solitude of an evergreen forest for a mile and a half. The trail climbs and switchbacks up another steep grade. Hinsdale Trail offers its own challenge of rocks, roots and rough log bridges. It eventually leads you to Route 63 and back to the parking lot.

CHAPTER 33

RUSSELL-ABBOTT STATE FOREST

Russell-Abbott State Forest has to be one of the best-kept biking secrets in the state. Located in Mason and Wilton along the Souhegan River, Russell-Abbott State Forest offers terrific biking.

The Russell-Abbott State Forest is an 886-acre tract of land that holds lots of adventure. On the property, the defunct Fitchburg Railroad bed is absolutely fabulous for biking. It's flat and the smooth gravel is in great shape. Before you take off, have a picnic at Pratt Pond. If you're a wildlife enthusiast or want to interest your children in it, the opportunity is here. Numerous waterfowl inhabit the pond, as well as occasional Great Blue Heron who stop to fish. The mountain laurel, if you catch it in bloom in June, is a bonus. Blueberries abound. The Souhegan River cascades over rocks in the river bed below as you drive above it on Isaac Frye Highway. This forest is truly a mountain-biking treat.

For additional activities in the Monadnock Region of New Hampshire, pick up a copy of *The Official New Hampshire Guidebook* at state information centers along I-93, write the state Office of Travel and Tourism at Box 1856, Concord, NH 03302-1856, or call them at 603 271-2343 to request a free copy.

Ride Information

Ride Level: All levels. Super for beginners—lots of flat trails.
Trail Distances: Varied. Over 10 miles if you ride all the trails. Could

Russell-Abbott State Forest

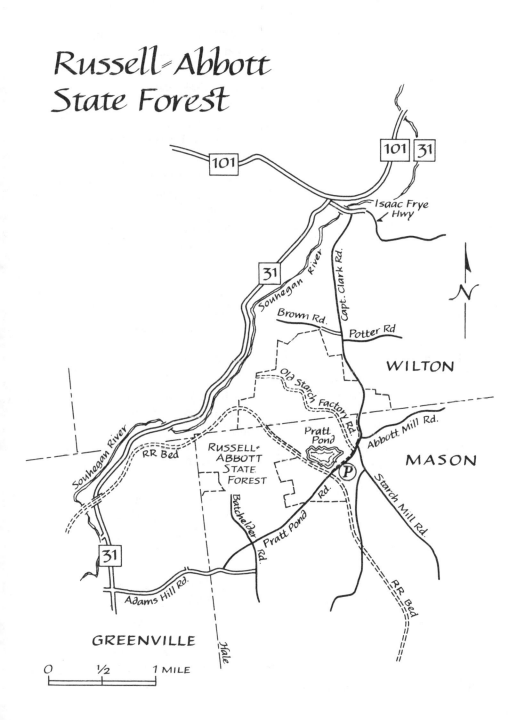

101

101 31

Isaac Frye Hwy

31

Souhegan River

Brown Rd.

Capt. Clark Rd.

Potter Rd

WILTON

Old Starch Factory Rd.

Souhegan River

RR Bed

Pratt Pond

RUSSELL-ABBOTT STATE FOREST

Abbott Mill Rd.

MASON

P

Batchelder Rd.

Pratt Pond Rd.

Starch Mill Rd.

31

Adams Hill Rd.

RR Bed

GREENVILLE

Hale

N

O   ½   1 MILE

be expanded substantially if you ride on the town roads or continue on the railroad bed.

Trail Descriptions: Flat. Railroad bed has no ties, smooth gravel.

Highlights: Wildlife. Picnic area. Serene pond. Super biking.

Start: Heading west on Route 101 in Wilton, take a left on Route 31, then a left on Isaac Frye Highway, right on Captain Clark Road for 1.4 miles to Starch Mill Road sign. Continue straight a short way then bear right on Pratt Pond Road to the railroad bed at Pratt Pond. Park on the right. It's gated, but riding is permitted.

Note: There is no admission fee charged. Stay away during hunting season.

Ride Options

These rides are out-and-back trails rather than loops.

1. Brown Road. A short, easy ride, Brown Road is 2 miles out-and-back starting from Captain Clark Road. This road looks like a driveway. You see a red barn. As you ride down the paved road you'll travel between a house on the right and the red barn on the left. Then the road becomes gravel. A sign says "Road Closed." The forester for the region said to ignore it—it's state property. It's a super road. At the gate a mile in, stop. It becomes private property there.

2. Fitchburg Railroad Bed. (This is where you parked your car.) It doesn't come any better than this folks. There is a gate at this entrance, but biking is permitted. It's flat, smooth gravel. Perfect. Go out and back as far as you'd like.

3. Old Starch Factory Road. This 7.5-mile out-and-back trail is a nice ride. You may encounter some mud during the spring as it crosses several streams.

4. Town Roads. The town roads—Captain Clark Road, Pratt Pond Road and Batchelder Road, for example—do have light car traffic, but are still super for extending your biking mileage.

CHAPTER 34

ANNETT STATE FOREST

T his forest fools most. The assumption is that this state forest in Rindge is little more than a picnic area. It is a picnic area—and so much more. Miles of trails and gravel roads nearby offer not only super mountain biking opportunities, but other activities as well. A short walk brings you to Hubbard Pond where birdwatchers and fishermen are in their glory.

The 1,300-acre forest was donated to the state in 1922 by Albert Annett, an industrialist from nearby Jaffrey. Annett State Forest is one of the state's oldest preserves. During the Depression the Civilian Conservation Corps built fire roads, reforested red pines and created many of the hiking trails at nearby Mount Monadnock. The fire roads, which form the network of trails in the forest, are generally easy riding. The forest floor, quieted by pine needles "under wheel," fosters a time to commune with nature, inhale the pine scent and appreciate the beauty of a mature, red pine forest.

For additional activities in the Monadnock Region of New Hampshire, pick up a copy of *The Official New Hampshire Guidebook* at state information centers along I-93, write the New Hampshire Office of Travel and Tourism at Box 1856, Concord, NH 03302-1856, or call the Office of Travel and Tourism at 603 271-2343 for a free copy.

Ride Information

Ride Level: All levels.

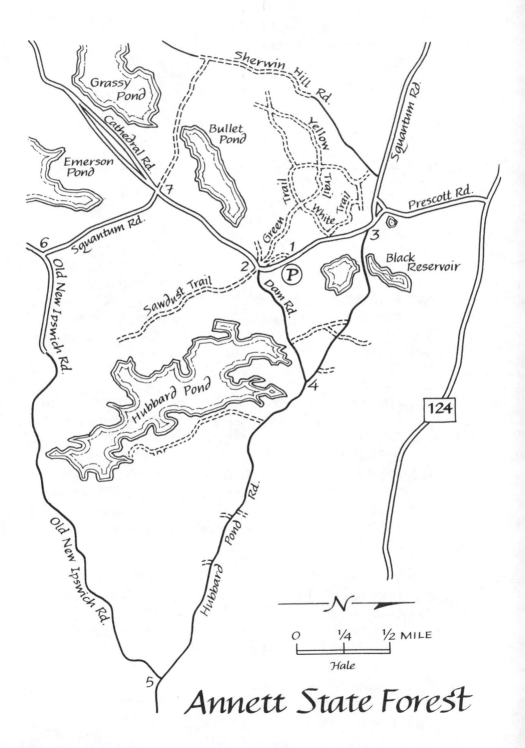

Annett State Forest

Trail Distances: Varied. Over 20 miles if you ride all the trails.
Trail Descriptions: Generally flat. Some rolling areas. Steep on occasion. Single-, double-track trails, and paved.
Highlights: Wildlife. Picnic area. Pond and dam.
Start: In Jaffrey Center, go east on Route 124 for 2.2 miles, turn right on Prescott Road. The road changes names, stay on Cathedral Road. The Wayside Park is .4 mile from Cathedral Road on the left. Park on the road if the gate is locked.
Note: A small admission fee is charged weekends at the Annett Wayside Park.
There are many trails that lead onto private property. Please stay off private land. Forest property is marked with blue paint.

Ride Options

These rides are out-and-back trails rather than loops. Intersection numbers are used on the map to better communicate.

1. Annett Wayside Park Loop. A short, 2.5-mile loop ride. Start from the parking area, go to intersection 3, 4, 2 and back to parking at 1. **Caution:** A bridge on the intersection 4 to 2 stretch near the dam is in ill-repair and not passable. You must walk your bike. Don't go screaming down this road and let it catch you by surprise.

2. Old New Ipswich Road Loop. A 6.7 mile loop that's partly on paved road and then gravel road. From the parking lot, go to intersection 2, 7, 6, 5, 4, 2 and back to 1.

3. Hubbard Pond Road. This road is a gravel road that is not maintained. A few hills will slow your progress, as will some erosion, but for the most part, this 2-mile stretch is easy pedaling.

4. Sawdust Trail. This spur road rolls through quiet wilderness until you reach the end of forest property—about a mile out. The blue blazes on trees alert you to the beginning of private property.

5. Color-marked Trails. For intermediate riders, a maze of trails fall between Sherwin Hill Road and Cathedral Road. A nearby inn grooms the trails for cross-country skiing. They're all color-coded and easy to follow.

About the Author

Barbara Rafte

Linda Chestney began her cycling career on a red Schwinn with no gears. But in the flat plains of the Upper Midwest you don't need much more. Schooling and family eventually brought her to the East Coast. Here she learned about a new cycling sport, mountain biking.

Chestney now puts thousands of miles on her sport touring bike and mountain bike while cycling the backroads of New England.

Chestney is a professional writer who has published articles nationally, regionally and locally. This is her second book. Her first book was *Cycling the Backroads of Southern New Hampshire*. She is publisher for Nicolin Fields Publishing.

She recently earned a Master's degree in Nonfiction Writing at the University of New Hampshire.